WHAT'S WRONG WITH MY THINKING

?

HOW ABUNDANCE THINKING CREATES BETTER OUTCOMES, MORE CASH FLOW, AND TIME TO ENJOY

RICK SCRUGGS, CLU, CHFC, C(K)P

ISBN-13: 978-1-957651-53-8
Library of Congress Control Number: 2023916325

Designed by *the*BookDesigners

INDIE BOOKS INTERNATIONAL®, INC.
2511 WOODLANDS WAY
OCEANSIDE, CA 92054
www.indiebooksintl.com

*To all my mentors, clients, and friends who have
imparted their wisdom and experience
to make my life's journey more enjoyable and fun.*

CONTENTS

PART I

Negative thoughts and a scarcity mindset can be a deadly combination for a private business owner. Time and again, I have seen the power of possibility thinking and an abundance *mindset* generate the energy, creativity, and courage to drive results. Abundance thinking, backed by financial integrity, is a powerful formula for the most aspiring ambitions. Now that is something worth thinking about. As a private business owner with your HIGO (house in good order), you can create a bigger, better financial outcome for you, your family, your employees, and your community.

1

WHY WHAT YOU THINK
IS SO IMPORTANT

John Wooden, the greatest college basketball coach of all time, once said, "I believe one of my strengths is my ability to keep negative thoughts out. I am an optimist." Wooden recognized the power of possibility thinking early in his career. That abundance mindset helped his teams win ten national championships while at UCLA.

Running a great private business is a lot like coaching a championship team. Success begins when you think like a winner.

When running a business, you have a lot on your mind. Yet how often do you think about what you think about? Or consider how you make decisions?

If you have your head down, are captive to the unremitting external demands on your time and energy, and looping through unproductive or habitual thought mazes, you may risk being blindsided. When you are not paying attention, considering the angles, or soliciting new and different perspectives, you are at best, hazarding shortsightedness.

At worst, you could be missing critical data that could imperil your business and your personal future. As the leader of your company, the plan for your own future affects the firm's prospects in countless ways. As the vanguard of your company's outlook, you must reach for a higher perspective to champion a compelling and substantial vision.

BEWARE YOUR BLINDERS

To do this, it may be helpful to consider the ancient tale of the six blind men in India. Each approached from a different direction when introduced to the great beast for the first time. The first blind man came from the front, felt the squirming trunk in his hands, and declared, "This feels very like a snake." The second approached from the side, moving his hands across the rough, large expanse, and exclaimed, "No, it's like a wall." Another came upon a thick, enormous leg and said, "I find it very like a tree." Standing beside him, the fourth blind man grabbed the enormous, flapping ear, "No, no, no, it's like a large fan or a carpet." The blind man who felt the sharp, pointed end of the tusk said, "Just as I suspected, it's like a spear." The last of them grabbed a swishing tail and said, "It's exactly like a rope."

Snake. Wall. Tree. Fan. Spear. Rope.

Each had a bit of the picture though not one chose an elephant. To learn the truth, it often takes putting all of the parts together. In this story, each man touched only one part of the enormous pachyderm. Piecing together the full picture means considering different perspectives and expanding your viewpoint. That takes open-mindedness, listening, collaboration, and discernment.

THE BUSYNESS OF YOUR BUSINESS

Effective people jealously guard their most precious assets: time and energy. The most innovative, effective, and productive entrepreneurs in the world have mastered the paralyzing hindrances of perfectionism and procrastination, according to Dan Sullivan, author of *The 80 Percent Approach*. According to Sullivan, the first time we do anything, it's 80 percent of the way there—and 80 percent of the time, that is good enough. First-time results may be great, but in our minds, we judge them to be only 80 percent of the way there because they are not complete. Sullivan maintains that it is a matter of quickly getting that first 80 percent done. It becomes an innovative way to focus on productivity and results that can transform how you think, communicate, and execute.

Think about this: how much time and effort do you spend working *in* your business versus working *on* your business? If *your* focus is totally consumed on the unrelenting issues of today, who is thinking about next year, five and ten years from now, or your personal transition/exit strategy? Great leaders always have a trained eye down the road, scanning for threats and opportunities. They do this by creating and updating plans for their company's stability and security, allowing them to position it for strength and to poise it for growth. That takes the kind of thinking that includes deep dives (soul searching) and flights to 30,000 feet (big picture).

HOW BIG IS YOUR FUTURE?

For most entrepreneurs, their businesses do not come with instructions. Yet like in life, when something does come with instructions, people are reluctant to read them. Business owners build their enterprises via the magic formula of LH/HW (*long hours, hard work*). Many started their business after they had an entrepreneurial seizure on a Friday night and found that instead of working for someone else for forty hours a week, they could work for themselves eighty hours a week and empower change.

Then one day, after years of breaking through multiple ceilings of complexity, they realize they need to create and train an entrepreneurial team—or the firm will never achieve what might be possible or even be sustainable. That's because LH/HW is not the solution to combat the complexity inherent within multiple areas, such as company growth, regulation, transaction growth, taxes, tariffs, industry regulations, and other aspects of business.

Then there is the law of unintended consequences, whereby you may change or improve something in one corner of your business activity that affects or influences something in another area in unforeseen ways. This requires coordination of seemingly disparate efforts.

CEILING OF COMPLEXITY
Private & Family Business Owners

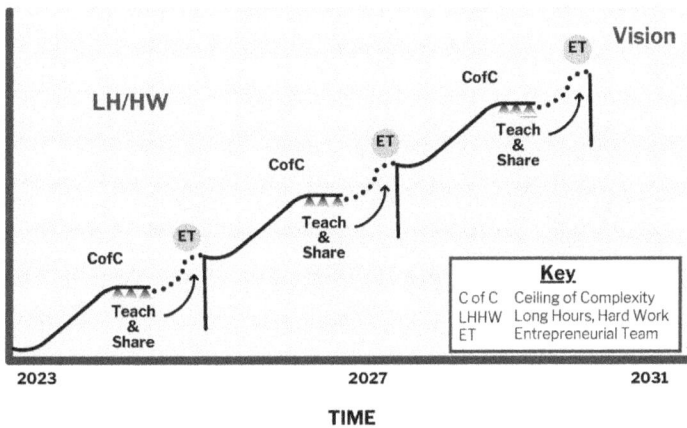

There are two hundred thousand private businesses in the United States worth $25 million or more, and ten million private and family-owned businesses generate between three and seventy million dollars in annual revenue. It is projected that more than half of those businesses are owned by baby boomers (all of whom will be sixty-five or older by 2030) whose plans for transition/exit may fail.

Approximately five million businesses are operating without a clear road map to the future, and a significant number will appoint or hire someone to take over, but those plans barely work. Why? The "pick someone" plan, whereby a successor is hired approximately twelve months before the owner exits, is not enough time. When it comes to passing the baton of your legacy, "the final test of greatness," that is cutting it too close. By identifying or adopting a "protégé plan" three to five years earlier, you create the opportunity to coach, mentor and shape your successor and delegate while the safety net (that would be *you*) is still in place. It gives your management team a chance to gel and hit their stride as a team. Those businesses who are not getting collaborative advice about continuity, success(ion), transition, and exit planning will heed the directive of poet Dylan Thomas who urged elders, "do not go gentle into that good night."

GOING GRACEFULLY

Your business is going to transition. Owners who do it well (go *gracefully* into that good night) can become wonderful ambassadors in the community by serving on nonprofit boards or by otherwise sharing their time and talent through philanthropy. Business owners can provide for their loyal and dedicated employees and ensure employment in the community for years beyond their tenure by ensuring their firm's financial stability and developing a culture that will endure. A successful transition will give you both the financial rewards you seek and the peace of mind accompanying a good hand off. It frees you to pursue passions and avocations long deferred to your work—the baton-pass is the final test of greatness.

DRAW FROM THE WELL

"Five years from now, you will be the same person you are today except for the books you read and the people you meet," according to author and motivator Charlie "Tremendous" Jones, who inspired millions at personal and professional development gatherings over fifty years. The well of information and ideas is vast, especially today, and forward-looking business owners will create the time to keep learning and expanding their knowledge beyond their business sphere by studying executive management, strategic planning, and leadership. They will create a board of trusted advisors and develop a cadre of professional friends and colleagues who can provide counsel, ideas, and synergistic introductions.

It really *should not* be lonely at the top. Yet too many business owners operate in isolation. They also tend to compartmentalize their advisors, who deliver input from silos without windows for collaboration. This can lead to unintentional harm to the company by good people who just need a wider lens. The result may engender a disservice to the owner's personal future. It is a miscue that can be quite costly.

By promoting transparency and bypassing competitiveness, bringing professional advisors together to collaborate on your behalf can be a winning strategy at the annual or even quarterly "audit" meeting. (Remember the six blind men and the elephant?) Connecting key players to contrast and compare their respective components (accounting, legal, technology, insurance, human resources, real estate) encourages big-picture insight that can lead to cost-savings and innovative solutions—and possibly expose vulnerabilities, the Achilles heel. Together, your team of advisors can create a brain trust that is focused on your company's success. That is *winning; that is an abundance mentality.*

ABUNDANCE THINKING

Often, we do not pull back far enough to be able to see what's wrong with our thinking. One way to do this is to look out over the next ten years. Multiply your annual gross sales by ten and add a little more because you will surely have growth. Next, calculate annual pre-tax profit in the same way. With the two aggregated sums, you are now looking at a bigger picture. Think about:

- Who does this impact?
- How does it affect key stakeholders such as your workforce, key employees, family, and community?

- How will you make the most of that revenue so you can look back and know you made a positive difference?
- What more is possible with all those resources?
- Start today to formulate a 10x Plan.

This first step exercise will start you on the path to embarking on abundant thinking and developing an environment of prosperity thinking within your business.

Coach and encourage yourself to "open the box" of your mind and let other thoughts flow in. We utilize *Time to Think* by author Nancy Kline as a process for owners and their teams to listen to their inner guidance as they continue to develop and refine their vision for the future. Seek books and courses to help you grow and expand your mindset. Be open to collaboration with others who can advise and support you. Learn and apply new ways of approaching your work. Ask for help!

TIME TO THINK

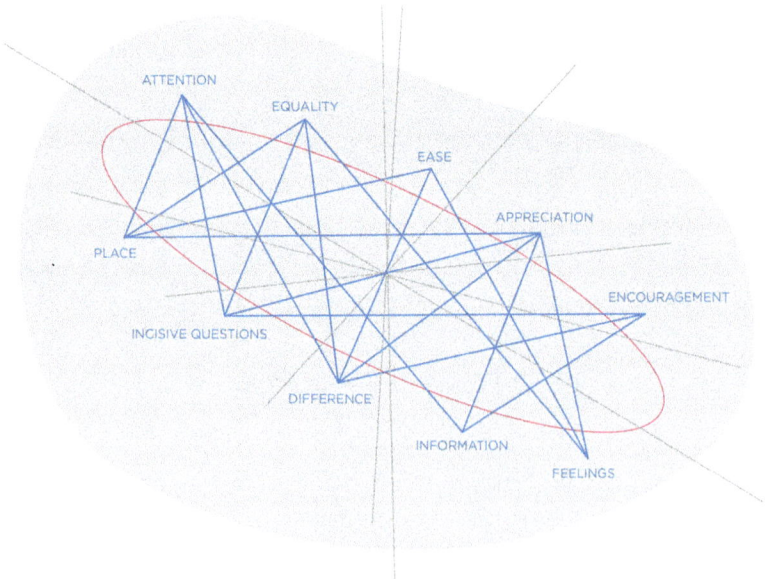

APPLYING POSSIBILITY THINKING

Why What You Think Is Important

1. Reflect on what you are thinking about and how you make decisions. Are you paying attention, considering the angles, and soliciting new perspectives? Revisit your long-term vision and consider how well-poised you are to achieve it practically. Then determine your intentionality around it and whether you're focusing enough on it every week.

2. Beware of blinders and potentially limited perspectives. Seek different viewpoints, solicit advice, and collaborate with colleagues inside and outside your business. Read. Ask for advice, and then really listen. Seek out experts and retain advisors.

3. Discover how much time you work *in* your business versus how much time you work *on* your business.

4. Have a written succession, transition, and exit plan strategy. Work on building an entrepreneurial team and a thinking culture companywide. Try to ingrain your thoughts with the idea that your baton-pass is the ultimate project to build a great legacy and your final test of greatness.

5. Dream about the company's big future—and your own. Think about what you want to manifest when the day comes that you're ready to embrace new pursuits.

Crystallize your vision and be able to succinctly share it with others who can encourage and support you.

6. Invite and align your closest advisors and consultants into your plans. Encourage internal and external team members to cross-fertilize by sharing information and ideas on your behalf.

7. Cultivate an abundant thinking mindset and promote prosperity thinking throughout the firm. Find clarity on questions about what you want to accomplish for your business and the kind of legacy you want to leave, both inside and outside of your life's work. Figure out ways to make a positive difference that will mean the most to you now and in the future.

In his classic, *Think and Grow Rich,* Napoleon Hill states, "We must have definiteness of purpose to have a great journey." This is sound wisdom: *definiteness of purpose.* Something that you must create for yourself. No one else will create it for you, and it will not create itself. Keep in mind you cannot aim too high.

SOMETHING TO THINK ABOUT

2

FIRST, WRITE IT DOWN

Before you go on a guided tour of how to turn your thinking into more cash flow and time to enjoy life, you should meet your tour guide. After all, what gives me the authority to share this advice with you? Like all entrepreneurs, my journey has had its ups and downs, with many twists and turns.

In 1973, during my freshman year of college, while I was home for winter break, my father died playing tennis on Christmas Eve morning at age fifty-eight. No goodbye. The next few days were spent planning his funeral, holding the service, New Year, and returning to school. It was difficult for me to process that holiday season because it was time to go back, take my exams, and carry on. There were no written instructions. I have some insights to share today with time, experience, and perspective.

My father was a World War II army veteran who shipped out on October 8, 1943, to Ireland and later to England in training for D-Day. His battalion had three companies and three landing craft boats. In one of life's ironies, on D-Day morning, June 6, 1944, his boat's engine wouldn't start, and his company would not land on Normandy for nine more days. The following five and half months were spent fighting the Germans and building Bailey bridges across France into Belgium for an eventual crossing into Germany. By Thanksgiving, there was a belief that the war might end soon. Hitler's surprise attack on December

16, 1944, in the Ardennes Forest began the Battle of the Bulge, which ended that thinking.

Over the next forty days, the US Army soldiers and Allied troops demonstrated courage, selflessness, and a willingness to sacrifice their lives for freedom and defeat of the Nazis. There were more battles after the Bulge; however, that victory changed the course of history. Only those soldiers who lived through the Bulge could describe that Hell. In another of life's ironies, the soldiers' winter gear had been sold on the black market in Paris because everyone thought the war would be over that fall. That winter was one of the coldest in Europe in over one hundred years. The casualties from the cold and trench foot were unimaginable.

My father's group crossed the Rhine after the Bulge and into Germany and final victory. When he returned home in December of 1945, he did what all the other veterans did; he went to work and became part of the greatest generation.

I don't believe he nor the millions of other veterans saw themselves as the greatest generation; however, after the Great Depression, the devastation of Europe, and the horrific Pacific war, building a future was all that mattered now. He never discussed the war before his death.

His story has taken me almost fifty years of reading, reflecting, listening, and visiting the beaches of Normandy to realize it can take a long time for self-awareness to emerge where we can understand our drive. We all are here today because we sit on the shoulders of those who came and sacrificed before us. Our visit to the blue planet is short, so by seeking clarity, we can decide what we want our future to be, knowing there is no guarantee of the outcome.

After the war, my parents lived a debt-free life except for a mortgage. They paid cash, and it wasn't until later that they established credit that they paid off every month. My father's career began in sales in Chicago in 1949. My mother had been a school-teacher before the war and she continued teaching and later became a librarian. I have an older sister, Diane, who was born in 1947.

My father was sold life insurance soon after Diane's birth, which he bought and paid for until his death. My parents saved for our college educations and straight teeth. It was not until the fall of my senior year, three and half years after his death, that I realized for the first time how my parents' work life, financial discipline, planning, and savings provided for our family's well-being. My father's life insurance provided the capital for my mother to maintain her lifestyle and dignity. She paid off the mortgage and worked as a librarian until her retirement. She then lived financially independent, traveling, volunteering, and grand-mothering until age eighty. Then the ravages of Alzheimer's took her mind until her death at age ninety-four.

A FORTUITOUS MEETING

By the spring of my senior year, I had interviewed multiple companies in many industries before deciding to work in the financial industry, specifically life insurance sales. I learned firsthand how financial integrity affects more lives than our own. Helping people to anticipate and plan for financial independence became my vision and purpose. Close to graduation, confident and determined, I was all set to join a life insurance company sales organization when I ran into a classmate getting ready to do the same thing. He told me I needed to call his dad, a general manager in Baltimore. When I called him, he encouraged me to contact a general manager in Virginia, Harrison "Chief" Nesbit, who I immediately called. Within a minute of our call, Chief asked me, "How old are you?"

"Twenty-two," I replied.

"Well, son," he said, "You don't stand a snowball's chance in hell of doing this job, so go do something else, and when you are thirty-five, come back."

Undaunted, I told him, "Sir, I am calling you out of courtesy. I'm *doing* this."

Two weeks later, I met Chief and his organization. His first question that morning was, "Are you coachable?" I said, "Yes, sir." I believe that answer was crucial and applies to all of us. At the end of the day, Chief offered me the career opportunity, and it was a seminal moment that changed my thinking and the trajectory of my life. Chief Nesbit became my mentor, friend, and champion for growth, abundance, and prosperity. He had an uncanny ability to ask tough questions designed to make you think. You see, he knew he could only help somebody if he could create an environment for them to think, and thus enable them to discover what they wanted by tapping into their innate wisdom.

Chief taught me that you could move mountains by asking good questions, tough questions designed to make you think and propel you to take action. That same first day, with the job offer, he gave me a book to read, which I did that night. I called the next morning to discuss the impact it had on me. He asked, "What do you mean?" I said, "Page 16, 38, 99, and 120." Chief said, "You read the book?" I said, "Yes, sir. That's what you asked me to do." He told me to come to his house for lunch the following day, and I quickly learned that many had been given the book, but few had read it. Following directions and being open-minded to wise counsel can be game-changing. Making those two calls without hesitation were early examples of "follow through," a concept I wouldn't grasp until years later.

Chief used to call me during those early years at five thirty in the morning: "How'd your goal setting go this morning?" Thinking big was a part of Chief's core: he wrote daily goals for achieving success, and his motto was to *get activities accomplished first thing in the morning*. He started making calls to CEOs and business owners between five and six thirty a.m. because he knew the gatekeepers would not be there, but the leaders would be. He coached others to strive for something bigger than themselves so they could impact their families and clients. Chief believed that thinking big mattered in changing people's hopes and dreams. Chief's clients were banks and corporations who bought corporate-owned life insurance for their executive benefits and their balance sheets.

After five years of sales experience and good success, I had an opportunity to become a minority owner and invest in a securities firm with a seat on Wall Street. This was my introduction to the stock market and investing. I quickly learned that 49 percent ownership with other minority owners is not 51 percent and control. Over the next year and a half, I realized if I wanted to do things my way, I had to start my own firm. I knew two local business partners who leased me space and postponed the rent for six months. I had my "entrepreneurial seizure" as described by Michael Gerber, the author of the *E-Myth Revisited*.

YOUNG, BUT NOT DUMB

With that break, I was off to "Ready, Fire, Aim," and I started Financial Designs, whose mission was calling on private and family-owned business owners. My father was thirty-nine when I was born, so I grew up around older adults. I was comfortable with these seasoned company owners who were more likely to need our new firm's services. While calling on the owners and asking questions, I continued to experience and learn that the owners' other advisors, accountants, and lawyers were not addressing the issues I was bringing up. We discussed buy-sell agreements, retirement plans, estate plans, key employee coverage, and other critical issues. This later became the Business, Continuity, Success(ion), Transition and Exit Planning (BCSTEP) business of Financial Designs.

The advice model was broken for these private and family

business owners. I was also part of the problem. Everyone was operating in their own silos (and silos have no windows). I was conducting business planning and was seeing how disjointed and incomplete it was for most of the companies we called on. Those companies were exposed to vulnerability, and it was clear that no one was giving them a cohesive, aligned perspective on their exposure. I read Chris Mercer's book, *Unlocking Private Company Wealth*, where he revealed a key observation: Business owners had not assigned an investment percentage of their business value to invest for a winning game plan.[1] He called it the 1% Solution. The answer was for an owner to annually pay 1% of his business value for advice and solutions. We realized we were also the problem as advisors because we were delivering our advice from a silo. Remember, silos have no windows. Today we work with owners who want to create a more abundant future, take massive action, and have time to enjoy it. Financial Designs' role is to help tear down the silos.

My mother, the librarian, had instilled in me a love for books and reading. So, I widened my perspective on business management, finance, leadership, succession, and planning. I took classes and attended seminars, hungry to digest everything I could about what makes companies flourish in good times and bad. Our firm grew because we offered integrated advice that was unique in the market. We held our own symposiums for clients and prospective business owners. Over the years, we grew knowledgeable in business planning, consulting, and helping expand clients' opportunities and minimize risks. This was long before I understood Black Swans (Nassim Taleb).

KINDLING PROSPERITY

Note: Time To Think—Forty Years Later

I can confidently say that we have helped more than one hundred private and family-owned business owners rest easier at night and dream bigger dreams. We helped them make better decisions by offering Time to Think (Nancy Kline) and challenging the status quo.

We take pride in knowing that their stability and prosperity has impacted their employees and families. We believe private and family businesses affect their communities' quality of life.

We have seen companies broaden their vision and achieve success they didn't think possible because of focus, determination, and abundance thinking. We hope the perspectives we share here will encourage you to find new ways to think about your business. Our goal is to ignite a spark and garner enthusiasm and commitment to your company's limitless prosperity.

POP QUIZ ABOUT YOUR THINKING

Think fast: are you more imaginative (right-brain dominant) or logical (left-brain dominant)?

As important as right-brain thinking is, as the center of possibility and creativity, it will not transform your dreams into reality. It is why a plan in your head is not a plan. A written plan is necessary; you must engage some left-brain moxie. You'll likely need several plans to articulate your overall strategic plan: financial, marketing and sales, manufacturing, operations, human resources, legal, and leadership.

To achieve vision with clarity, you will need to power up both sides of that incredible brain of yours. Clarity allows us to make wise choices. Great plans are aspirational, with sky-high visioning combined with real-world practicality. They set direction and define focus. By prioritizing initiatives, they align the energy and efforts of your workforce and advisors into the plans and projects with the highest potential for strategic success.

"Discernment, influence, and being a go giver changes the future."—David Berg.

YOUR PERFORMANCE SCORECARD

Your widely shared plan becomes the platform for tracking goals, evaluating performance, and benchmarking your success. You can turn it into a dashboard that becomes a tool for regular progress reports; this simplifies and enhances your ability to communicate your focus. Your team will know where you want to take the company and how they can contribute. It brings everyone together and becomes the touchstone for decision-making when new ideas or opportunities are presented. NETMA (nobody ever tells me anything) is the most dangerous acronym to discover applied to your business culture.

Before you dive into designing the specifics of your plans, however, it is a good idea to test your acumen on key management issues: delegation, hiring and leadership development, prioritization, communication, and financial strategy. So, in advance of zooming in, it is instructive to take a wide-angle view. By reading this book, we propose that you are in the right place to begin assessing your perceptions and actions around some of your key performance indicators (KPIs).

THE ART OF LETTING GO

Delegation is less about the mechanics of who, what, when, and how to parse your workload than your resolve to let go and mentor. Allowing others to step up to develop their knowledge and abilities helps you and deepens the knowledge bank of the entire company. If you could free up just ten hours a week, think about what you could accomplish in those extra 520 hours a year—equivalent to a three-month sabbatical. Do you think that has the potential to move the needle on one or more of your biggest aspirations?

THE PEOPLE PIECE

If you concentrated those hours solely on the people part of your puzzle, it would be time well spent. Few factors have as much effect on your success. As a leader, one of your paramount goals should be to recruit and develop the best talent you can possibly afford. Updating hiring practices, refreshing recruitment strategies, and developing incisive interview skills are vital team-sport activities, and you will want to involve as many as possible from within and outside the company. Ideally, your emphasis on hiring high-performing employees would parallel a sustained effort to grow and develop leaders individually and as a high-functioning team. Team-oriented employees are one of the biggest and best investments you can make for your future.

HIGHER ORDER THINKING

Focusing on what matters is a game-changer. In work, as in life, everything boils down to essentials when a crisis occurs. Clarity leads to wise choices. It can be extremely challenging to pull yourself out of the chaos of the now to discover your true north. You may find you will need some new tools and fresh approaches to change how you think about your business and what matters. Once you do, you will likely have a higher perspective that keeps a trained eye on your big goals and your endgame. How do you think that might change how you address your work?

DECODING MESSAGES

Communications vex the most seasoned leaders in all walks of life, in all manner of businesses. Including context and purpose with instructions helps convey your full intent, allowing people to see how their work serves the greater whole. When you first define and then endeavor to communicate your "why" in immediate or long-range scenarios, you build allegiance to your higher purpose. Direct, pointed messages work well with your customers and team; brevity and simplicity help make them readily understood. Think about what you are talking about. Can perfecting your messages improve your communication skills?

MESSAGE NOT DELIVERED

With our increasingly fragmented attention spans and the noisy demands on that limited attention, we have a crisis in comprehension. A message sent is not necessarily a message received. Putting aside differences in culture, education, and generations, the odds are still stacked against our ability to convey our full intent. Assigning a little more effort to check understanding is a good first step, followed by evaluating any of your own limiting perspectives and assumptions. After you have refined your key messages, adopt redundancy in all ways and means possible— be sure everyone is clear about what is important to you. Can you remember a time when miscommunication caused a major snafu—and how it could have been avoided?

UNDERSTAND YOUR NUMBERS

Consider how well acquainted you are with your company's financials. Are you closely tracking the things most contributing to your firm's success? Though not all those metrics for achievement are directly revenue related, having your financials current and in good order—with accrual accounting in place—puts you in a commanding position to build company value and take advantage of new opportunities. Financial and business success planning are integral to maximizing your company's value and securing your personal financial independence. Are you prioritizing time and allocating resources to the things that matter most?

TOWARD MORE AGILE THINKING

Next, we will explore more completely the pillars of success that can help you achieve clarity and boost your effectiveness across several disciplines. It's not complicated. It's simple. But that doesn't mean it's easy. You'll have to be open to new ways of thinking and being. You must acknowledge that it all starts with your personal and professional growth and willingness to improve.

Financial Designs is responsible for over $1 billion in invested assets, 401(k)s, IRAs, nonqualified investment accounts, cash values, and life insurance death benefits. We've worked with hundreds of private and family business owners who have taught us how small changes can make a huge difference. How basic planning and foresight can transform an owner's outlook and a company's prospects. How widely differing businesses encounter the same management hindrances and roadblocks. And how easily savvy yet pressed owners get shifted off course from their best intentions and highest aspirations.

THE GREATEST REWARD

It is a privilege to work with intelligent, hardworking, and dedicated entrepreneurs to help them craft plans and systems that bring resolution and order to weighty matters. "Uneasy is the head that wears a crown," said Shakespeare's King Henry IV because owners have a lot of responsibility on their shoulders—and a lot of people depending on them: their employees, their customers, their families, and their communities.

As a business owner, I grapple with the confusion and complexity of matters outside my wheelhouse (technology infrastructure, for instance). When I strive for clarity, I can make better, wiser choices that can potentially lead to success. Bringing clients direction and peace of mind is the greatest reward of my work. Our success in this has been inestimable. I calculate it by the deep intrinsic rewards of seeing client companies achieve their potential, business owners manifest their dreams, and stakeholders share in the ensuing prosperity.

APPLYING POSSIBILITY THINKING
First, Write It Down

1. Engage both sides of your brain to materialize your goals: dream big and focus your thoughts on a written plan. Align the company's energy and efforts into projects with the highest potential for strategic success.

2. Share your plan widely and consider turning it into a dashboard so you can monitor progress, motivate others, and communicate your intentions.

3. Delegate some of your workload and free up time for aspirational projects and higher-order thinking. What could you accomplish in the equivalent of three months?

4. Rise above the distractions of the day and pull yourself out of the chaos to discover your true north. Find some new tools and fresh approaches to change how you approach your workday to home in on your overarching priorities.

5. Recognize that many people depend on you to be your absolute best. Bravely address the confusion and complexity of matters outside of your comfort zone, knowing you probably just need more information or to seek assistance.

6. Learn from my personal life experience to plan for the unexpected and be prepared for the unimaginable.

Build your company's safety net and prepare to rise above resistance, knowing that even in challenging circumstances, you can flourish.

7. Broaden your vision and find new ways of thinking about your business. Rekindle the passion and excitement of earlier days when you thought anything was possible because it is. Do you believe it's time to expand your horizons?

SOMETHING TO THINK ABOUT

PART II

The more you share your vision, philosophy, and aspirations for the firm, the more you impel a solid legacy of success when you step aside or sell; at the same time, you're building the company's value.

3

DELEGATE THE SMALL STUFF

"Begin with the end in mind" is sage advice for a private business owner. That is Habit Two from Stephen R. Covey's *Seven Habits of Highly Effective People: Powerful Lessons in Personal Change.*[2]

Here is my question to you about the end: Will you leave your company ten toes down or ten toes up?

Your answer to this is moot because either way, you will leave. But you can walk out on your terms with all toes down, or they can carry you out, toes up.

Ask yourself, what kind of legacy will I leave?

Here are some other questions to ponder: Are you actively pursuing your key priorities for the company? How about your highest aspirations? Does your leadership team have clarity and commitment to your vision, values, principles, and culture?

The degree of empowerment you provide to others directly correlates to their confidence and ability to carry on in your absence, even if you're just on a tropical jaunt off the grid.

The key thought for a business owner is to delegate the small stuff on your plate. And believe it or not, most of what is on your plate is small stuff.

SAY NO TO THE SMALL SO YOU CAN SAY YES TO THE BIG

Successful delegation begins with a common, though perhaps not-so-simple premise: Hire people who are more intelligent than you. Then you must invest in them by developing, nurturing, believing, and giving them wings. The difficulty for most business owners is that they often find themselves running in deficit mode—and it takes a significant commitment of time and energy to find the right hires and then mentor them. So, if you're habitually running in deficit mode, attending to what management guru Stephen Covey calls "urgent yet not important" matters, you're probably missing this "important yet not urgent" priority.[3]

REALLY, WHAT ARE YOU *DOING*?

In Greg McKeown's book, *Essentialism*, he reveals the power of saying no so your yes has a more significant impact and garners respect from your team.[4]

What would you do with that time if you could free up ten to twenty hours a week? What kinds of projects could you undertake to really move the needle on your key business objectives? The secret may first lie in discovering how you spend your time each week. Initially, you might identify the time buckets that categorize your management, such as time spent on strategy, business development, administration, client service, learning, leadership, etc. An honest assessment, perhaps by keeping a daily time log for a few weeks, might clarify where you spend your most precious resource.

You may find it helpful to start each day by planning your work hours; start by metaphorically pouring them into time buckets. Divide your time into not ten or twenty cylinders but into just two or three cylinders. Take care, now: if you don't properly pour your time into the right cylinders, you'll spill it all over the floor. The time then evaporates and is irrecoverable. The biggest cylinder is the bucket that holds the most important things you can do that day, and the other one or two buckets are the things you can delegate.

Whether you are aware of it or not, there may be underlying insecurities around parsing out your workload. You are successful because you have been effective and mastered myriad aspects of your business. Maybe you've been too busy to take stock of what you're doing and why you're doing it. Or could it be that you don't know what you'd do with all that extra bandwidth? It's often easier to let go of the mundane (and what's comfortable) when you have identified what energizes, empowers, and drives you toward stretching your goals.

SHARING THE LOAD

You may have compelling reasons why you must personally undertake everything you're doing. However, chances are you have team members who could adeptly offload you, given a bit of mentoring and collaboration. Motivated employees are eager for more responsibility, participation, and time with their leaders. You have hard-wrought wisdom and experience to impart; share it to benefit others, yourself, and your company. You want to foster the environment of employees asking for more responsibility.

Inviting others to participate more in day-to-day management allows you valuable time for mental planning, exploration, and creativity to design and actualize the future you want for yourself and your firm. Let your newfound intention to recapture ten to twenty hours a week guide you: your visionary projects are calling.

With family-owned businesses, you'll get the same results if you do what the previous generation did to succeed. Yet most companies would like to grow. Take Floyd, chairman of Sonny Merryman, Inc., a school bus sales distribution company in Virginia and a commercial bus sales operation. Floyd's father and mother built the company with teamwork. Sonny left at 4:00 a.m. every Monday and returned home at 4:00 p.m. on Friday, made sales calls throughout Virginia, built long-term relationships, and manned the front back home.

Floyd and his sister Pat have taken the organization to the top of their game and are not finished. They hired Caley Edgerly as CEO and president, and Floyd himself became chairman. Pat has recently retired and continues to serve on the board. Floyd has a dedicated team and a chief financial officer, Angelo Castanes. They have assigned solid managers to be responsible for each division and department. Floyd knows their key metrics, shortcutting his need to read lengthy reports and allowing him to communicate with Caley if he wants more information. This macro-level perspective allows him to communicate and respond to his leadership team, significantly benefiting the company. Floyd has time to enjoy his business because he hired A-Players, and Caley and the company are growing a 10x future.

SHARING OWNERSHIP

Frank Martin was a go-getter type of entrepreneur with high energy and street smarts. In 1979, he co-founded Threaded Fasteners, Inc. (TFI) of Mobile, Alabama, with his brother-in-law, Steve Sholtis. A good leader, Frank had hired a great core team and mentored them for thirty years. Yet he didn't know how to pass the baton financially when planning his retirement. He knew his managers did not have the resources to buy him or Steve out.

He could sell the business to a strategic buyer or even guide the employees in borrowing funds to finance the sale, though he knew he wouldn't get the full value for the company. Notably, adding to his predicament, Frank had a generous nature and abiding loyalty to his team, who had been so integral to the company's success.

A NEW FIRM TAKES FLIGHT

Daryl Bryant, founder of 6th Street Advisors, knew Financial Designs' works with private and family business owners and employee stock ownership plans. Daryl enlisted Rick to collaborate, learn, and grow while helping TFI remain locally owned and operated. An ESOP seemed like a good solution.

Daryl and Rick presented the concepts to Frank and the management team. The idea of employee ownership proved to be the winning solution for TFI. Billy Duren became president and created a next-generation team that has grown revenue, profits, locations, and employee ownership value for over fifteen years. The acronym WIIFM (what's in it for me) combined with IP (irrefutable proof) are Billy and his team's goal.

Financial Designs and Daryl conducted quarterly retreats, monthly calls, management meetings, and introductions with other professional advisors to bring the ultimate collaboration to the table. It takes a team of advisors working with a business and its management to achieve the best results.

GIVE IT UP TO TRADE UP

Building a stellar team to carry a company into the future isn't always easy, though the practical and intrinsic rewards are often substantial. Successful delegation doesn't only help leaders; it helps their companies, too. According to a 2015 Gallup study of the entrepreneurial talents of one hundred forty-three CEOs on the *Inc.* 500 list, companies run by executives who effectively delegate authority grow faster, generate more revenue, and create more jobs.[5]

Dan Sullivan, founder of The Strategic and best-selling business author, asserts that for a company to grow exponentially, "It doesn't need *you* managing—it needs *self-managing.*" Face it: one way or another, you will move on someday. Have you thoughtfully considered who will fill those big shoes of yours? Or the legacy you'll be leaving when you go? By beginning with the end in mind, you can let that vision guide you as you work toward the goals you have for yourself and the aspirations you have for your company.[6]

APPLYING POSSIBILITY THINKING
Delegate The Small Stuff

1. Strategize your endgame now. Have you considered the legacy you'll leave, and are you working toward your priorities and highest aspirations? Beginning with the end in mind may help you clarify what you need to do now to work toward your vision for your company and yourself.

2. Hire smart people, then mentor and empower them. Hiring well and mentoring high-performing employees takes commitment, time, and energy. Attending to this "important, yet not urgent" priority pays dividends.

3. Discover how you presently spend your time, so you can identify what may distract you from your key business objectives. Consider keeping a time log or tracking your daily activities by sorting them into time buckets and delegating less important tasks.

4. Identify what energizes, empowers, and drives you toward your stretch goals so you will be motivated to free up time to focus on that. Share your wisdom; step up mentoring and collaboration so you can offload your responsibilities while empowering others to expand their knowledge and experience.

5. Build your company's value by inviting others to participate in day-to-day management. By sharing your vision, philosophy, and aspirations for the firm, you propel a solid legacy of success when you step aside or sell.

6. Study how successful entrepreneurs work more *on* their business than *in* their business by empowering their teams, sharing responsibility, and strengthening future helmsmanship. Take a cue from Frank Martin, who adeptly ushered his company to employee ownership, resulting in impressive growth after his retirement.

7. Concentrate on the rewards of delegation, knowing that companies run by executives who effectively delegate authority grow faster, generate more revenue, and create more jobs. Striving to get a company to be self-managing is the best and fastest way to achieve exponential growth.

SOMETHING TO THINK ABOUT

4

HIRE THE BEST, FORGET THE REST

When asked to reflect on the success of the company he dropped out of Harvard University to found, Bill Gates of Microsoft said this: "In the long run, your human capital is your main base of competition. Your leading indicator of where you will be twenty years from now is how well you're doing in your education system."

In short, hire the best people you can find and support them to achieve their best.

People are the foundation of any great organization. Great people create great products and services, attract great customers, and build great companies.

So, okay, simple: hire great people. *How hard can it be?*

It's nothing short of excruciating for most companies, comprising their biggest handicap and most elusive goal. If some hires aren't the right fit or up to the job, it will hold your business back. When you solve this main problem, things will open up. Your company can't grow until you master the people side of the business. Great family businesses avoid the three-generation shirtsleeves to shirtsleeves dilemma because they master the people part of the equation.

THE COMPANY YOU KEEP

Building a great team is one challenge that will hamstring you if you don't get it right. It also constitutes one of the most significant blind spots for all owners because the air gets thin at the top. You're truly alone unless you're surrounded by the best and the brightest.

You won't have people around to challenge you, to learn from you by asking why you're choosing the moves you are making. People who really strive to understand your motives, your mistakes, your values, and the factors of your success. Team players who will tell you the truth and share an unvarnished perspective, even one they know may be unwelcome. Loyalists who still question your decisions and challenge your approaches (with respect, naturally), thus providing you with a genuine reflection and an honest read on the tenor of the rank and file. (Hint: if your direct reports only have good news for you, you're probably missing some mission-critical insight.)

One of the biggest deficits for a private or family-owned business is not finances, it's human capital. Time and treasury spent building a stellar team are investments that pay rich dividends. When you build a culture of truth speaking to power (you), you have vested players who clearly understand and share your vision. When people don't know where a leader, or an organization, is ultimately headed, they default to WIIFM—*what's in it for me*—because it's the natural law of self-preservation. Fundamentally, it's about all of you believing in something bigger than yourselves: a shared aspirational purpose.

ARE WE HAVING FUN YET?

It's also about having *fun.* Maybe not the laughs-a-minute kind of fun; this is *business fun.* You know, the challenge of working together toward a common goal. Fun creates energy. Energy creates magnetism. Magnetism attracts people who are attracted to the right vision. Fun is energy-giving, not energy-zapping. It comes when team members tap into their unique abilities and achieve something they didn't think was possible.

So how can you wake up every day with that energy of fun? What we're all looking for on some level is that energy: the energy of excitement. Commitment. Inclusion and acceptance. The energy of presence: Being right where you want to be, where you know you belong. The drive that comes from reaching for goals: The pursuit of happiness. A quest that author Joseph Campbell called the archetypal hero's journey, a roadmap for which is his oft-quoted adage, "Follow your bliss."[7]

Ultimately, it's also about creating value in the world. Making a difference, a positive contribution, in whatever way you want to define that. This is how you create true and lasting success on both the corporate and personal levels. The trick is to determine the size of the gap between your dreams and the state of your life, business, or values, then work to close it. So, you will need to get people on board with that. The key is acting early to map your aspirational goals; this allows you to move forward with less tension and more purpose. Stepping back and empowering your team is only possible when you hire the right people and demonstrate courage.

PEOPLE POWER, PEOPLE PRESSURES

No business is successful without the support of many people: Top-notch companies are comprised of first-rate people. Few decisions are more important than hiring and developing high-performing employees who meld into a high-functioning team. Dan Sullivan, author of *Who Not How: The Formula to Achieve Bigger Goals Through Accelerating Teamwork*, says, "Treat your employees like an investment, not a cost."[8]

It's also important to remember that a bad hire can be destructive to your company—and morale. So, if you've determined that there is an unsolvable mismatch with an employee, resist the tendency to "give it time" or "let it play out." Like cancer, it's only going to grow, and it is going to affect the systems around it as it does. Remember, *not* acting has consequences, too.

EVEN THE BEST TRANSITIONS ARE TRYING

Turnover is expensive at every level and at both calculable and incalculable costs. According to *Forbes,* both direct and indirect costs should be considered when assessing the fallout of hiring and onboarding a new employee. Some direct expenses are for recruiter fees (about 20 to 30 percent of the first year's salary), advertising, interviewing costs, signing bonuses, relocation reimbursement, and administrative costs for things such as pre-employment tests and reference checks. Administrative time and expenses might include preparing training materials, benefits enrollment, and accommodation purchases for special equipment or supplies. The training costs for training the new hire can be significant, too, particularly when the new employee isn't producing at full capacity during training.[9]

Since it takes two to three months to replace a knowledge worker and another month or two to get them fully up to speed, the more subtle, though no less impactful effects of turnover include downtime, lost revenue from reduced productivity or sales, and distraction from other priorities as you, the trainer, and the trainee work to help them become fully functioning in their role. More employees than the new hire share the burden of the transition, and it can affect the morale of busy employees who may miss their former colleagues and resent losing productivity during the transition. Acknowledging and expressing appreciation for your team's extra effort during the onboarding process should go a long way to smoothing out the rough patches of a transition.

RECRUITING (AND ONBOARDING) IS EVERYONE'S JOB

Human resources personnel are only a functional part of finding, assessing, hiring, training, and enculturating your new superstar employees. Every touchpoint the candidate or the new hire has within the company makes an impression and influences their perceptions about your workplace. The best things you can do to raise the bar on hiring:

1. Spend more time on the front end of your hiring process and assess your systems.

2. Analyze the "why" behind your hiring and ensure it is clear at the organizational level and to the candidate.

3. Learn great interviewing techniques, and train your team to ask the right questions and to listen intently.

4. Discover the science of work style personalities and determine what works best for your organization and the position at hand.

5. Consider including personality testing in your hiring process (there are many books, courses, and instruments for this) to measure thinking style, verbal reasoning, numerical reasoning, self-management, and coachability.

6. Commit to a robust onboarding process, involve several employees, and personally check in often with the new hire to ask how it's going. Listen and respond with action to what they tell you.

Financial Designs recommends clients utilize profiling tools such as the Kolbe A Index, ProfileXT, Manny Steil's Personalysis, and InnerZone assessment tools. They look at how current and prospective employees think, communicate, collaborate, decide to act, and fit in with your firm's culture.

Great recruiting goes beyond finding someone with the functional ability to do the job. One Financial Designs client had a highly capable chief financial officer who left the company to pursue another opportunity. Before he left, he recommended that the firm hire someone with a strong accounting background. They hired someone with strong technical knowledge; however, developing this individual into a true CFO took three years. It was a classic case of someone with the smarts but lacking the skills and systems to grow faster.

When you hire great players, they know their role and how they contribute to the bottom line. You can't hire great people if you don't have a compelling vision and culture. The important thing to remember is not to compromise your vision because transforming your current reality into your ambition will never be devoid of obstacles. Your goals are slipping away when you compromise in large and small ways. And goals are the stepping-stones to attaining a vision. You need the best possible team around you, which means elevating hiring practices from being a pain to prioritizing them as a privilege.

GREAT LEADERS NEED COUNSELING, TOO

In working with private business owner clients, our team has introduced Time to Think (Nancy Kline) with all companies. The sessions begin when team members are asked one question, and we listen—no feedback. Our role is to listen.

"They're probably the best listeners you've ever encountered," one of Financial Designs' long-time clients said. "There's a quip that goes, 'Know the difference between a coach and an advisor? Well, a coach asks you twenty questions and gives you no answers, and an advisor will give you twenty answers without asking a single question.' Now, Financial Designs does neither yet blends the two approaches. It's an entirely different sort of approach. Unexpected, even surprising, but it is really very effective—and powerful."

Leaders *need* that kind of deep listening, even when they aren't aware of it. Eric Schmidt, author of *Trillion Dollar Coach*, a biography of Silicon Valley C-level advisor Bill Campbell, tells how some of the smartest, most successful executives on the planet accelerated their careers with Campbell's coaching. Many reluctantly accepted the help; some even rebuffed and later relented. The value of having someone to ask you penetrating questions, coupled with attentive listening, cannot be overstated. The listener needn't have brilliant solutions or incisive advice other than occasionally sharing an observation, reflection, or prompt to get the speaker to dig deeper, scan wider, and shoot higher to discover the ideas that lie within.

APPLYING POSSIBILITY THINKING

Hire The Best, Forget The Rest

1. Resolve to solve the people part of your puzzle. When you solve this portion, things will open up. Make mastery your aim in leadership: become a great recruiter and an inspiring mentor.

2. Embrace the fact that time and money invested in people pays rich dividends. Decide you will build a strong culture with a shared aspirational purpose, working together to achieve something big.

3. Hire smart people, then mentor and empower them. It takes commitment, time, and patience. Aim to create a collegial atmosphere of teamwork and fun on the journey upward.

4. Believe in people, though resist the tendency to put off the inevitable when you know it's a mismatch. A wrong fit creates a situation that will likely worsen over time and could potentially affect other systems and people because nonaction has consequences, too.

5. Know that transitions are costly in more ways than financial. Be involved in the onboarding and training processes. Encourage several people, not just the primary trainer, to become involved in helping the new hire learn, enculturate, and get up to speed.

6. Elevate the stature of the process of recruiting and onboarding new hires companywide. It's an important objective that ideally involves the whole business. Strive to raise the bar on the whole process by involving staff in learning new interview techniques and investing in the new hire's success.

7. Consider what qualitative attributes you seek in candidates for the position. Investigate adding pre-employment assessments to your process because functional skills and experience are only half of the equation.

8. Find someone to confide in with whom you share your concerns, confusion, and ideas. Leaders need a sounding board and a reflective listener to process thoughts and test-flight concepts. You may be surprised at what develops from a free-flowing dialogue of thoughts and ideas.

SOMETHING TO THINK ABOUT

5

FOCUS ON WHAT REALLY MATTERS

What age are you going to be when you die?

Think about it. Everybody's got a number, so how did you arrive at yours? Health, family genes, or guess? Okay, let's change the game. Picture a tailor's measuring tape: 120 inches long, encompassing the longest life span. So, here's the exercise. Pinch the hash mark corresponding to your current age and look back to zero. That is your past. Next, with your left forefinger to your current age, move your right forefinger forward to indicate your age when you retire. Finally, grab the tape at your "forecast" date. What do you think? The years to get it right are finite if you want to enjoy a post-retirement longevity bonus.

If you aspire to establish a company that will last a thousand years, you have a millennium mindset, yet a mere one hundred years to build its strong foundation. The purpose of this exercise is to prompt you to think differently about the future and to consider what's possible. By shifting your focus off the unrelenting "now," you may find you have a greater sense of urgency to start planning for tomorrow and a pressing need to get started on the dreams and ambitions you have for your life and your enterprise.

"What you think about, you bring about," according to *New York Times* best-selling self-help author Bob Proctor, who proselytizes the law of attraction. So, what are you thinking about: the mundane or the aspirational? You're mapping out the destination when you spend time at work looking out the window, contemplating what you want and where you want to go (and take your company). Puzzling out the best journey to get there now becomes your essential work, fueled by the clarity of your enlivened ambition. It's guaranteed you will end up in a better place—possibly one that exceeds your expectations and imagination.[10]

DON YOUR THINKING HAT

Why not encourage yourself to be circumspect by exploring ways to think about your situation and the company's outlook differently? Creative problem-solving starts with thinking outside of the box. Next, you may want to consider the method developed by Edward de Bono in his classic creative-thinking treatise, *Six Thinking Hats,* a book I highly recommend learning. The book proposes a way to segregate and channel your analysis into different perspectives, allowing you and your team to engage various dimensions of a subject or issue through objectivity, devil's advocate, creativity, optimism, caution, and emotion.[11]

De Bono proposes that thinking is stimulated to engender new approaches and alternatives by deploying the figurative thinking hats first singly and then in a sequence. It's a way of turning off your critical, analytic brain for a while, encouraging you to suspend judgment, tap creativity, and consider what else is possible. The six areas of focus include:

SIX THINKING HATS

White Hat: Stands for neutrality, objectivity; characterized by facts and figures. Prompts: *What facts do I know? What information do I need, and how will I get it? What's most important?*

Red Hat: Signals emotion, anger; characterized by feelings. Prompts: *How do I feel about this? What are*

my hunches, intuition, and impressions telling me? How attracted or repelled do I feel by this idea?

Black Hat: Represents solemnity and criticality, characterized by caution and negativity. Prompts: *Is it true? Will it work? Why won't it work? What's the worst-case scenario? What are the weaknesses?*

Yellow Hat: Epitomizes positivity; characterized by hope and optimism. Prompts: *What are the good points? What are the benefits? Why is this worth doing?*

Green Hat: Typifies growth and expansion, characterized by creativity and ideas. Prompts: *What are some possible solutions? What other alternatives are there? What other ways are there to approach it?*

Blue Hat: Exemplifies calm, cool abstraction; characterized by focus, control, and organization of thinking. Prompts: *Have I covered all the bases in my approach to thinking this through? Have I been objective in my process? Where do I want to end up in my thought process? Has my process produced clarity, or do I need to restructure or rerun it?*

Source: *Six Thinking Hats* by Edward de Bono.

Playful yet effective, the metaphoric thinking hats can be an incisive way to compare facts and opinions, synthesize new ideas, identify solutions, plan, and improve processes. Why not conjure Big Hairy Audacious Goals to make the most of the thinking hats approach? Also known by the acronym B-HAG, the term was coined by Jim Collins, author of *Built to Last,* the second of five books in the *Good to Great* series. According to Collins, the idea here is to imagine visionary goals that are more strategic and emotionally compelling. It all begins with "blue-sky thinking," a form of creative brainstorming that posits: "If there were absolutely no limits, no judgments, and no consequences, where could your imagination take you?" The sky's the limit.[12]

The trick is to think about what matters most to *you*. What would you like to see happen? What do you care about? What is the effect you want your organization to have? Is it about the money? Is it about prestige? Is it about being number one in your industry? Is it about helping your employees retire with financial independence? Is it about making a significant contribution to your community?

TURNAROUND TIPS

A wonderful client and friend, Jack Eckert, now deceased, was president and COO of McDermott International in New Orleans. Jack was a nuclear engineer and spent most of his career building Babcock & Wilcox (a nuclear company) before it was acquired by McDermott, an oil and gas deep-drilling firm. When Jack was asked to go to New Orleans, he had no experience in oil and gas operations, international negotiations (Russia), and the complexity of a multinational firm. I would visit Jack in New Orleans annually, and on that first visit, I asked how it was going, and he responded, "We lost $280 million last year." So, a year later, when I returned and asked the same question, he said we made $280 million, over a $560 million difference. I said, "You must have changed the company's direction 180 degrees." In his humble voice, Jack responded, "No, just two degrees." "What?" I exclaimed. Jack replied, "Well, I knew nothing about oil and gas, so I had to let those who did do their job while providing support, input, and decisions when asked or needed." What a direct, non-conflicted solution. Jack mastered the art of listening and zeroed in on what was essential to the company's success. Usually, you just have to give people the freedom and resources to make wise choices.

Another great CEO was Phil Asherman. Phil (now retired) was the CEO of Chicago Bridge and Iron, which he cleverly explained was not in Chicago, did not build bridges, and did not use iron. The company had relocated to Houston, where the organization's 54,000 employees worked globally on complex projects involving hundreds of millions of dollars in construction and annual revenues exceeding thirteen billion dollars. Phil learned success involved leading people while expecting high performance, feedback loops, and not operating on hearsay. He believed culture is vital to company success. Phil epitomized the highest ethical standards and safety-first principles. His employees' lives mattered. He understood there was no reward without risk; however, he believed you should operate to minimize as much risk as possible. Talented people held to the highest standards of accountability and collaboration can deliver exceptional results. These two industry giants did not run private and family businesses; however, their business principles apply to any market or business.

SKIRT THE NOT SO OBVIOUS

Even if you are conscientiously focusing on your long game, there can be unplayable scenarios that aren't readily apparent. The team at Financial Designs knows these as "black swans" after a theory developed by former Wall Street trader Nassim Nicholas Taleb, who uses the metaphor as a nod to a historic precept that decried black swans to be nonexistent because all known swans were white—until they weren't. In short, Taleb's theory is that highly improbable, impossible-to-forecast events can have dramatic if not drastic, consequences. For countries, economies, and companies alike, these can be internal or external circumstances that cannot be predicted or anticipated. (Think 9-11, the 2008 financial crisis, the 2016 election, Brexit, COVID-19.) According to Taleb, the secret lies in your company's "antifragileness" response to an event: Will it propel demise, exert resiliency, or capitalize on the opportunity? *Can you take the blow, even grow, and come out stronger?* [13, 14] That's becoming antifragile (Taleb).

"Beware the blinders," says Nassim Taleb. Note the hubris of Titanic captain Edward Smith, speaking of the White Star's *Adriatic,* a precursor to the fateful liner he skippered: "I cannot imagine any condition which would cause a ship to founder. I cannot conceive of any vital disaster happening to this vessel. Modern shipbuilding has gone beyond that." Before that, in 1907, he said, "I never saw a wreck and never have been wrecked, nor was I ever in a predicament that threatened to end in disaster." Later, after his *first wreck* (the Titanic), a United States senator said of Smith, "Overconfidence seems to have dulled the faculties usually so alert."[15]

While the age-old adage *forewarned is forearmed* doesn't apply to black swans because they are unpredictable, it guards against complacency and perhaps recalls another trusty dictum to plan by: *expect the unexpected.* Business, as in life, is chock-full of risk. What's important to remember is that you can hedge against the unforeseen by building resources and fail-safes that can sustain your company through an unanticipated rough patch.

CONSTRUCT RESILIENCE

Buzzy Coleman is someone I considered both a client and a friend. When the nonprofit foundation for the National D-Day Memorial in Bedford, Virginia, unexpectedly ran into financial difficulty during a major construction project, Buzzy and his company Coleman-Adams, a family-owned construction business, stepped up to solve the challenge. After working in the construction industry his whole life, he had the financial resources to complete construction. He said, "It was my patriotic duty to finish it." He was able to give back because he had a well-planned transition/exit strategy; *you gotta make good to do good.* Today the National D-Day Memorial stands as a lasting tribute to the sacrifice of the men and women on that epic day.

PC: Ryan Anderson/National D-Day Memorial Foundation

But as the famous radio announcer Paul Harvey used to say, here is the rest of the story. Earlier in the company's history, when a major recession hit the construction industry in the 1990s, the economic fallout threatened Buzzy's construction company and its ability to do business.

The company had tapped its lines of credit, and banks were requesting new signature guarantees. "We hadn't been paid for a major project we'd just completed, and our bonding company wanted us to pledge our personal assets before accepting any new work," according to Buzzy. "For a builder, things could not have been worse."

When consulting me about their predicament, the company's work over the years with Financial Designs paid off. Their established life insurance policies had more than a million dollars of cash value. In their hour of greatest need, they had the resources to pump in cash, satisfy the bonding company, pay creditors, revitalize, and keep moving forward in uncertain times.

According to Buzzy, "Instead of slowing down, we were able to stay aggressive and keep the employees working, and it gave us cash to operate on so we could make the paychecks on Friday and pay our bills to the subcontractors so they could keep working. Those resources pulled us through, and I still have my company. That's my idea of a pretty good investment."

Buzzy then decided to expand Financial Designs' role to develop a continuity and success(ion) plan for Coleman-Adams. Financial Designs quarterbacked the team of advisors, legal and accounting, while holding employee team meetings off-site to have open conversations and share ideas. Financial Designs recommended key person life insurance policies as an incentive for key people to remain with the company, through the leadership transition to Buzzy's sons, Clif and David. When Coleman-Adams got hit by the 2008 Great Recession, the company had the cash reserves to make it through again. Proper planning prepares companies for unplanned events.

MANAGE ISSUES EARLY

Sometimes those niggling issues that are bothersome but hardly seem important to focus on today may lurk in the shadows. Subject to conscious neglect or unintentional oversight, they can potentially burgeon into huge snares that could have been averted. Financial Designs recommends safeguarding against denial by devising early warning systems to monitor and manage issues early.

Issues management is a reality that evolves from business maturity. As your company grows, often incrementally at first, the amplifying degree of complexity may take you by surprise when you're overly focused on immediate issues. If you're not paying attention or consulting others in a regular environmental scan of internal and external circumstances that directly affect your business, you could be caught out by something that reaches critical mass seemingly out of nowhere. You may need to keep your head on a swivel to continually recalibrate what's important and what threats and opportunities are emerging.

QUESTION SUCCESS

When offering a new client engagement, Financial Designs' advisors employ a visual metaphor to help illustrate their unique consulting approach: Matryoshka dolls. Also known as nesting dolls, they are hollow, painted wooden figurines that separate, revealing smaller and smaller dolls placed one inside another. The advisors assert this portrays how they seek to delve ever deeper to discern a client's core values, true motivations, and highest aspirations. Pairing reflective questions with deep listening, they encourage people to explore vantage points seldom afforded by busy executives. The results can be transformative for leaders and their companies.

It's about keying in on what is most important to the principal. Consider one of Financial Designs' clients, a second-generation president, Greg Morris of AMG, Inc., a high-end machine shop in Lynchburg and Roanoke, Virginia, with one hundred thirty employees. Of paramount importance to this leader is to have every one of the company's employees retire with financial dignity and security. Like many companies, there is a 401(k) plan with match, quarterly cash profit sharing. However, their ESOP has been a key to their growth and prosperity. Every month, Greg openly shares operational and financial numbers so every team member understands exactly how the company is performing and what it means for their future. This provides an allied vision for (and vesting in) the company's success, helping employees understand how they contribute to its achievements.

The company has engaged in multi-year strategic planning with Financial Designs today to ensure growth and profitability.

PROMPTS FOR EXPLORATORY REFLECTION

Top Five Questions To Jumpstart Your Thinking

1. Over the years, who has been your mentor or somebody with an irrational interest in your success that has made all the difference in the world?

2. How many people within your organization have you thanked? If we were to construct your life's board of directors right now and put the names of people who've had the biggest impact on your life, what would those names be?

3. Is it important that your business remains locally owned and operated and continues to affect the quality of life in this community?

4. Are there concerns you have in recognizing that our visit on the blue planet is pretty short and that mortality is a hundred percent? Is there anything you'd like to ensure we put at the top of the list now? Were the odds against you, and yet you succeeded anyway? Could you share that with me?

You may employ project management, people management, debt management, and even weight management. How's your *thought* management?

MIND YOUR BUSINESS

Business continuity and succession, transition, and exit planning are critical in every business life cycle. Early in the business relationship with Robert Roberts (now deceased), we learned that what mattered most to Robert was hiring a talented, productive workforce and providing fair and competitive employee benefits and incentives. He founded EDM (Electronic Design & Manufacturing), which produces printed circuit boards for various high-technology products and systems marketed to a complex and competitive market. Discussions about business philosophy, entrepreneurship, and employee stewardship evolved into a solid benefits program for EDM, including group benefits, a 401(k) plan, corporate-owned life insurance (COLI), and other business benefits. Financial Designs, Robert, and GeorgeAnn Snead, president, had discussions surrounding success(ion) where the idea of an ESOP was introduced. Next, a team of tax, legal, and ESOP experts was brought to the table.

"The greatest single thing for us was having employees own the company," according to Robert. "Employees have a vested interest in efficiency and reducing waste. They're more concerned about making a good product and ensuring customers receive maximum service."

Robert maintained that because he viewed employees as the firm's most important asset, treating employees with the respect they deserve was a core value for him from day one. Thus, involving his team in the plan to share significant long-term benefits of the company's growth and earnings was a big part of his prosperous succession and retirement. Twenty years later, the EDM team and their robust planning continue to pay rich dividends: today, some employees are retiring with multi-hundred-thousand-dollar accounts from the ESOP, fulfilling Robert's goal to reward their loyalty and create their financial independence. When Robert retired EDM's management and employee team was intact and aligned for the future.

CULTIVATE A HUNDRED-YEAR MINDSET

Do you have a one-hundred-year mindset regarding your enterprise? Consider the story of the copper beech tree, which takes one hundred years to reach maturity. At its majestic pinnacle, it reaches fifty to eighty feet high with a broad, spreading canopy. Yet beech trees grow exceedingly slowly, and seedlings can take ten years to get two feet tall—twenty years to grow fourteen feet and forty years to scale just twenty-eight feet high. Amazingly, it may take the next forty years to grow just twenty feet to reach a mature height of forty-eight feet. Standing at the base of the sapling, it's hard to imagine it growing that big when it's just struggling to survive to two feet tall. Standing at the base of the eighty-foot, hundred-year-old tree, it's hard to picture the sapling from whence it sprung.

By employing a corollary to your company's growth, the metaphor may be apt. The grand old tree arguably had many challenges in its slow and patient journey to the sky. It had to face swaying in the wind to stimulate long-term root growth, producing permanent anchors against uprooting in a storm. A dearth of nutrients while it was young encouraged extensive root development, as its roots stretched out to build a wide and strong network to nurture the tree for decades. It likely faced floods and drought, bitter winters, and scalding summers. The threats were many, though skyward it rose.

The zenith of the copper beach tree's steadfast growth is mature simplicity. This is the penultimate achievement for private companies who adeptly conquer ascending levels of complexity. It is a state not generally attained without unwavering attention to what matters.

Starting a company requires grit, determination, and vision. There are many more adjectives to describe Melvin Hinton, an Army Ranger veteran who founded MH Masonry ten years ago. Melvin started the company at age fifty-seven without money, customers, or employees. His former employer had gone bankrupt, and Melvin now wanted to start his own company. Being a minority was irrelevant to Melvin because he is color blind. He simply expects each man or woman to be their best and deliver the finished product.

Melvin had developed relationships over the years where he delivered finished jobs to contractors and owners. They were now willing to extend credit and provide new projects to MH Masonry. Financial Designs began day one, holding Saturday morning meetings with Melvin and his partners, outlining the steps and goals they would need to implement for success.

They were coachable and wanted to win. Today, ten years later, and after multiple challenges, the company has delivered. Their benefits, retirement program, and Work to Win incentive plan all contribute to a winning formula for all employees. The best definition of winning is going as far as you can go and giving it all you have with your God-given talents without guaranteeing the outcome.

Chris Tharp, a third-generation owner, has demonstrated coachability, abundance, and breaking down barriers. He saw talented people and the market opportunity to end segregation in the funeral business. Today his owners are male and female and black and white. Tharp Funeral Homes is color blind also. They continue to work with Financial Designs to be a 21st century growth-oriented company.

To date, Financial Designs has worked with over ten, fifty-year old plus companies (500 years in business), learning, growing, and contributing.

APPLYING POSSIBILITY THINKING
Focus On What Really Matters

1. Consider the time left in your working life and how many years you expect to retire. Now imagine what may be possible and what you'd like to accomplish in both spheres. Question how committed you are to shifting attention from the unrelenting now to designing your future.

2. Explore ways to expand your thinking and discern deeper insights around your intentions for yourself and your company. You may want to try new approaches to channel your analysis into different perspectives, such as scrutiny, objectivity, creativity, optimism, caution, and emotion. To think big, be bold in your process.

3. Be mindful of *black swans*, those improbable and impossible-to-predict circumstances that may develop suddenly. Strive to build resources and fail-safes to sustain you and the company through an unanticipated rough patch. Hedge against unimaginable risk by building resilience and shoring up your financial foundation.

4. Manage low-priority issues that have the potential to burgeon into huge, inevitable snares. Safeguard against denial by monitoring and managing issues

early. As your business grows, stay aware of the amplifying degrees of complexity you will face and the need to recalibrate what threats and opportunities are continually emerging.

5. Resist the tendency to neglect to check in with and reevaluate your core values, motivations, and aspirations. Score yourself on how well you are navigating toward your true north. Adjust as necessary, either to expedite your progress or to redefine direction.

6. Remember, it's a marathon, not a sprint. Embrace the lessons of the copper beech tree, emblematic of mature simplicity attained by conquering ever-ascending levels of complexity. To cultivate resilience in all circumstances, uphold an abiding and resolute focus on what matters to you.

SOMETHING TO THINK ABOUT

6

COMMUNICATE THE RIGHT MESSAGE

A friend of mine, let's call him Andy, a successful entrepreneur who was eighty years old, told me he had hired a twenty-five-year-old to help manage his company. Although Andy was a seasoned executive with extensive knowledge and business acumen, everyone around him questioned the decision.

"So, why'd you do it?" I asked him.

"I just wanted to hire somebody smart and see what they could do to help the business," he told me.

"And how's it working out?"

"Well, when I communicate something to Jim, he takes my conversation and develops a written communication strategy that all can understand and execute. Plus, the written strategy becomes memorized."

"That's pretty interesting," I said. "Let's see; it's about delegating the message so it can be clarified and elevated to another level so people can do the work and see how it serves your goal."

It implies that you trust the person you're delegating it to and have confidence in their ability. By recognizing that they may do it differently from you, you also provide that it may potentially be carried out better than you would have done it. Suppose you have specific objectives for people, assignments, plans, and projects. In that case, it is your responsibility to convey the why behind your intent and, preferably, how it aligns with the greater vision. It is acutely misguided to assume people can contextualize how pieces serve the whole. Yet that knowledge empowers enthusiasm and purpose.

THE POWER OF WHY

In his seminal TED talk titled "How Great Leaders Inspire Action," Simon Sinek presents a model for persuasive communication. With over fifty-five million views, the incisive speech outlines the main precepts of his now-classic book, *Start with Why*. He explains what he calls the golden circle and why he considers it probably the world's simplest idea, yet one that explains why some leaders inspire while others do not. Why do some companies break out of a competitive pack in their markets, leaving others to eat their proverbial dust? In Sinek's words:

> *Every single person, every single organization on the planet knows what they do, 100 percent. Some know how they do it, whether you call it your differentiated value proposition or your proprietary process or your USP. But very, very few people or organizations know why they do what they do. And by "why," I don't mean "to make a profit." That's a result, it's always a result.*
>
> *By "why," I mean: What's your purpose? What's your cause? What's your belief? Why do you get out of bed in the morning? And why should anyone care? Well, as a result, the way we think, the way we act, the way we communicate is from the outside in. It's obvious. We go from the clearest thing to the fuzziest thing. But the inspired leaders and the inspired organizations— regardless of their size, regardless of their industry—all think, act, and communicate from the inside out.[16]*

The three concentric circles of Sinek's model are comprised of *Why, How, and What.* He posits that it is grounded in biology and corresponds to three major components of the human brain, influencing how we make decisions and what drives our behavior. The outer concentric circle represents the neocortex, which processes the *what* of our decisions: rational and analytical thought and language. The middle and center sections make up our limbic brain and are responsible for all of our feelings, he says, feelings like trust and loyalty. These areas are responsible for all human behavior, all decision-making, and they have no capacity for language. Ergo, we generally trust feelings (our gut instinct) more than data (our rational mind).

Sinek maintains that when we talk directly to the part of the brain that controls behavior, we allow people to rationalize it with tangible things we say and do (the *what* of facts and figures*)*. "If you don't know why you do what you do, and people respond to why you do what you do, then how will you ever get people to vote for you, or buy something from you, or, more importantly, be loyal and want to be a part of what it is that you do? If you hire people just because they can do a job, they'll work for your money, but if you hire people who believe what you believe, they'll work for you with blood and sweat, and tears. And if you talk about what you believe, you will attract those who believe what you believe."[17]

EMBRACING BREVITY

When your mother is a schoolteacher and a librarian, you talk a lot about language and develop a love of books. Consequently, my mother taught me that giving a twenty-minute talk is much more difficult than to ramble on for an hour. She encouraged me to think about what I wanted to communicate and to fine-tune the message to mature simplicity. When working on the sixth draft of a three-quarter page letter of engagement, I grin, knowing that my true goal is to pare it to half a page—and that she'd approve.

From Abraham Lincoln to Mark Twain to Martin Luther King, leaders who deliver short, powerful speeches and pen pithy essays make a bigger impression than the most loquacious orators or bombastic writers. You have plans to write and ideas to share. For the greatest effect, choose as few words as possible and strive to overcome complexity so they are read and clearly understood. In the age of social media that limits expressions to 280 characters and three-minute videos, your busy audience will appreciate your ability to write and speak succinctly. My mentor Chief Nesbit was quick to admonish me: "Never say 'baa baa' when 'baa' will do." It took me ten years to learn as a young man: just shut up and listen.

SEEKING SIMPLICITY

"Make everything as simple as possible, but not *simpler*," Albert Einstein said. In business, this probably equates to striving for ease of comprehension while retaining the full import of the message. In short, what we at Financial Designs refer to as *mature simplicity.*

One client had worked hard to map out aggressive yet achievable goals for his company. We coached him:

> "For the entire year, you are to talk about the company doing $20 million in revenue with $2 million in profit. We don't want you to worry about how you'll do it or that you've never done it before. And when people ask you how, you just say, 'Well, we're going to do these three things: we're going to bid right, we're going to show up on time, and we're going to finish what we start.'
>
> Just keep it simple. Your job is to ensure that people understand and are focused on every job they're working on: *Why are we here? What's going well? What needs to be adjusted?*"

Mature simplicity ain't always so simple. Steve Jobs fought the same battle during his whole career at Apple: one for simplicity, simplicity, simplicity. It was his call to arms if you'd like. Yet even though he strove for artless elegance in every endeavor, he was wise enough to continually seek feedback to affirm that it had been achieved: comment and criticism kept him objective.

SUCCEEDING THROUGH TRANSPARENCY

In organizations large and small, information can become a commodity. Some workplaces operate on the premise that whoever has access to the most information has the most power. In competitive environments, operational news and data are held closely and guarded jealously. The most common areas of withholding information are performance, revenue, internal processes, sourcing, pricing, business values, negative trends, and risk.

Transparency is about openness in business operations. The kind of honesty that encourages a free exchange of knowledge and ideas to empower employees so they are truly vested in the company's growth and success and have the kind of information they need to perform their jobs better. Transparency builds a culture of trust, with a foundation of strong relationships between employees and management. It helps you to model communication and enculturate the company's values. It engenders more collaboration, shared learning, creativity, and problem-solving, which can result in improved performance.

It works with bad news, too. Resist the inclination to hide it when something goes wrong. Be upfront about the issue: tell it all, express it directly. Know that you cannot control how people react, yet you can approach the situation with candor, clearly expressing that you do not intend to threaten or throw anyone under the bus. Your team will often respond to your openness and caring and work together to ameliorate the issue.

Your willingness to be candid yet caring when it is tough can strengthen loyalty if employees believe you are in it together.

You can encourage transparency through updates such as a periodic newsletter or briefing memo, hosting regular all-hands meetings, and directing managers to relay information to employees in their departments. Remember, however, that good communication is a two-way street, so permit people to be transparent without fear of looking foolish or appearing malcontent. By encouraging feedback, ideas, and troubleshooting, you're building a perspective that can provide valuable insights to trigger early-warning systems for operational deficiencies, issues management, and emerging opportunities.

APPLYING POSSIBILITY THINKING

Communicate The Right Message

1. Ask yourself if you are clearly conveying how everything serves your greater goals. Having someone to assist you in this may be helpful. Remember that context can be critical to reinforcing purpose and alignment with greater goals.

2. Be guided by the power of why in your communications. Center your thoughts and actions around the why of what you do and what you aspire to achieve. Write and speak about your why at all possible times.

3. Master brevity to heighten attentiveness and deliver a bit of punch to your writing and speaking. Consider

your audience, who is attuned to getting information in short missives and headline news.

4. Seek mature simplicity through ease of comprehension. Repetition is not nagging but useful in emphasizing your fundamental values and goals. Welcome comments and criticism, which help ensure the message sent is the message received.

5. Brave transparency in business operations to build a culture of trust. Learn for yourself how it facilitates collaboration, shared learning, creativity, and problem-solving, which combine to improve performance. Resist the inclination to hold back or delay bad news; as your greatest test of candor, loyalty can soar when you are forthright yet caring.

6. Make communication and transparency a company value. Facilitate the flow of information in your organization by proactively communicating through formal and informal channels. Encourage feedback, ideas, and troubleshooting through open and honest two-way communication.

SOMETHING TO THINK ABOUT

7

ASSUME NO ONE HEARD YOU

Irish playwright George Bernard Shaw famously said: "The single biggest problem in communication is the illusion that it has taken place."

Consider this situation. Playing outside in her backyard, a little girl falls and scrapes her knee. Hearing the girl's cries, her mother comes out, comforts her, and cleans and bandages the cut. When finished, she hands the girl a cookie and says, "Here, this will make it better."

A while later, she returns to find her daughter sitting on the stoop. Looking up at her mother through tear-filled eyes, the girl whines, "It's not *werrrr-king,*" while holding the cookie on her bandaged knee.

Is your intent clear for the messages you convey?

Is anyone really listening?

On both accounts, it's probably best to assume *not.*

CHECKING UNDERSTANDING

Not long ago, I helped a client, Brian, test both his communication aptitude and his employee's ability to take appropriate action. His industrial distribution company was being challenged: staff members in the warehouse were complaining about deliveries gone awry, late, or missing shipments, and incorrect packaging.

I told Brian to go out to the shipping dock and talk to Bill, one of his managers, about what needed to be accomplished to get things back on track. After he was confident that he had given thorough instructions, I told him to start to walk away and then turn around and ask him, "Hey Bill, just so we're both on the same page because I'm going to be out of the office tomorrow, would you confirm what I outlined?"

Brian regards Bill as a loyal, dedicated, and trusted employee. Yet he was stunned at Bill's response. "It was 180 degrees from what I thought I had explained," he said ruefully. "It was so 'off' I was dumbfounded."

Today, the management team at Brian's company has adopted the maxim: *Assume no one heard you.* They no longer presume immediate understanding; the managers now realize how difficult it is for people to execute on limited information.

Somewhere along the line, we've created an environment in business where it is not okay for people to ask for clarification. Employees are not encouraged to check understanding by asking, "Would you tell me more about that?" or "Can you tell me what exactly you mean by that?" Encourage questions and allow team members to reciprocate by permitting them to be candid and to field inquiries without fear of appearing foolish. As delegators, we have become too rushed to take a few extra minutes to get confirmation from people about the request or instructions— because the intended message may not be received.

PERCEPTIONS AND ASSUMPTIONS

You've undoubtedly seen those optical illusion illustrations where you see a picture, and the caption challenges you to see the *other* picture your mind does not readily perceive. You search for the alternate, and now you can see both, though perhaps you wonder why it took longer to see the second picture, realizing you may have missed it altogether if you hadn't been told it was there. Now, if someone comes along to view the drawing and first sees the picture you saw secondly, who is right?

Perception has the potential to complicate everything, especially in communication. Add in different cultural, language, and generational perspectives, and it's probably safe to assume no one truly listens to your words. Try to increase self-awareness: are you making assumptions about people, projects, and problems? Examine your perceptions and ask others how they view or comprehend them. Clarify to connect.

RELENTLESS REPETITION

Well before he became president, Ronald Reagan was known as "The Great Communicator." A charismatic orator, he campaigned with strong, clear messaging that cut through the rhetoric and became engraved in the public's mind through relentless repetition. Legend has it that during his countless speeches, reporters in the campaign press corps stood in the back of the room mouthing his stories and phrases in sync with him. The actor-turned-politician carefully crafted his script, studied it well, and stuck to it, repeating his key messages with unquestionable success.

Classical conditioning asserts that we learn most readily through repetition and surprise (shock). Advertisers and marketers know this drill well. Research suggests that redundant communications through different channels are highly effective in business. A joint study by Harvard Business School and Northwestern University found that managers who convey messages via emails, texts, and conversation (by phone or in person) get more attention and action from their teams. The findings conclude that for optimal response, "repackage and rerun" your key messages and vital requests.[18]

While some communications researchers differ on whether listeners best respond after three or seven times of hearing a message or directive, it's clear that repetition is a good thing when it comes to getting heard. In *How Google Works,* authors Eric Schmidt and Jonathan Rosenberg assert that "repetition doesn't spoil the prayer" because messages take about twenty times to sink in. Google management found that people are too busy to notice a key message the first several times. They become vaguely aware it may have significance, and when you're completely sick of repeating it, people are starting to get it. Being proactive in reminding people of your objectives (large or small) is highly effective, so for quick action, follow up to underscore your intentions. Squeaky wheels are very biased to results.[19]

DISTRACTIONS EQUAL INTERFERENCE

"Business is usually a team sport," says Stephen A. Schwarzman, author of *What It Takes: Lessons in the Pursuit of Excellence.* "There isn't one great person sitting there directing things. You can't run an effective business like that." Given that, if the play caller can't read (or worse, *misreads*) signals from the sideline, the whole team could be imperiled by muffed plays. When there is interference in the relay, check the strength of your signal and the accuracy of the reception.[20]

We've all had the experience when someone is trying to tell us something, but we can't focus on what they need to tell us because we have something else fully occupying our thoughts. When you sense this is the case, you might ask, "May we talk about this another time? I'm distracted by something else just now. I want to hear what you say, though I can't give it the attention it deserves." Similarly, if you're trying to converse with someone stressed or distracted, you can defer the conversation and plan to talk another time. Of course, it's always a good idea to approach colleagues with a simple "Is this a good time to talk?" Confirm attention before you begin.

INTRODUCE EMPHASIS

A great way to emphasize your message is to follow a formula professional speakers use to structure their talks:

1. Tell 'em what you're going to tell 'em

2. Tell 'em

3. Tell 'em what you told 'em

You can introduce your message conversationally with phrases such as, "I'd like to talk to you about (subject) and discuss (general overview) because (why)." If you talk about why it is important to you, you will likely heighten the receptivity of your listener. Providing context to the ensuing conversation helps the listener see the bigger picture and how their role fits into it. Engaging their interest and previewing the subject at hand prior to launching into your core message may be more effective at capturing and retaining their attention. By flagging your conversation as something meaningful to you, you are telegraphing your desire that they pay attention and respond in kind.

APPLYING POSSIBILITY THINKING

Assume No One Heard You

1. Resolve to take a bit more time and effort to think about what and how you want to communicate. Strive to be direct and incisive.

2. Check understanding so you are confident that the message you sent was received. Encourage clarification when giving people instructions, and if in doubt of their comprehension, ask them to share their understanding of the request.

3. Allow people to ask questions without fear of looking foolish or inept. Be relaxed and unhurried so you can take the time to discuss and clarify, emphasizing your desire to provide complete context and concept.

4. Search your own perceptions and question your assumptions to uncover any blind spots. Determine if you have rushed to judgment on people, projects, or problems. Ask others about their conclusions and perspectives. Clarify to confirm your own and others' understanding.

5. Employ redundant communications to get your messages out: use email, texts, and conversation to encourage action and alignment. Repetition is good, so assert your determination to be heard on anything and everything important to you.

6. Watch for situations when you or others are too distracted to have a productive conversation. Beg off politely to defer the conversation to when you can give it your full attention. Respect that you may need to offer the same courtesy to others if they are temporarily unable to concentrate on what you have to say.

7. Learn from professional speakers how to convey your message with an "intent sandwich" surrounding your core conversation with a good introduction and a restatement wrap-up. Providing context helps people see how they can participate in the bigger picture of the dialogue.

SOMETHING TO THINK ABOUT

8

UNDERSTAND YOUR NUMBERS

A farmer calls his business partner on the way home from the weekly farmer's market. "I've got good news and bad news. We sold out, but the sales barely covered our expenses, let alone our time and effort."

"Oh, boy," sighs the partner. "We're going to need a bigger truck."

The moral is if you're losing money on every deal, you won't make it up in volume. If you are merely referencing topline revenue, your profit line could be diving deeper and deeper into the red because you did not account for expenses or cost of goods.

I knew a company with its best gross numbers for two consecutive years but made no money. They had the sales and the revenue, yet due to a lack of certain control issues, they didn't profit from that hard work—in fact, you could call it a counterfeit success. Additionally, the way their business was structured, they were in line to pay corporate taxes twice and take a beating on their real estate holdings when they sold their land and buildings site. You see, it's not just about knowing your numbers; it's about knowing the *right* numbers.

If you have retained a CPA to develop your balance sheet, take time to have them explain it to you and ask them questions. Delve into the implications of your financial performance so you comprehend your company's gross versus net revenue.

Learn what metrics you need to know and how they affect your bottom line. Most of all, discover what key performance indicators (KPIs) most influence your company's financial picture and resolve to track them closely.

KNOWING WHAT TO TRACK

You can start by deciding what KPIs best reflect your company's performance: the metrics contributing to your organizational objectives. It's not the same for all enterprises; it is tailored to your business because you design it and it serves your company's unique goals. Reports generally address four main arenas: finance, internal processes, the customer, and learning and growth (innovation). Within that framework, your essential benchmarks might include any number of operational objectives within the categories of finance, sales, customer service, human capital, operations, legal, and internal systems.

Developing a scorecard of nine to twelve indices will give you a quick read on trends, strengths, emerging challenges, and how well you're progressing to forecast. Regular reports can provide insightful data on how well the business is achieving tactical, operational, and strategic goals. (Some teams color code their dashboards to correspond to green, yellow, and red for performance assessment with just a glance.) Updated weekly, this real-time gauge on business administration can be a powerful incentive for leaders and their teams, rendering a sense of control and unifying vision. It's also an early-warning system. Allowing you to address negative trends early can be invaluable for allocating resources and guiding strategic decision-making.

We discovered that Financial Designs' clients prefer to receive the reports either at the end of the day on Friday, which gives them the weekend to mull the results, or first thing on Monday, which prioritizes the week ahead and directs a deeper dive when warranted. The report is a topline overview;

the indicators represent multiple factors that can be further explored and analyzed.

IMPLICATIONS OF KNOWING THE SCORE

Business continuity and success(ion) planning is like a parachute: you'll never need it again if it's not on and in place when needed. It is never too soon to think about your transition and final exit strategy. Regrettably, some closely held business owners are pressed into it by a life event. Fortune favors the prepared company because business continuity planning directly informs company value. Your plan should analytically and philosophically comport with your vision and goals for the best outcome.

Valuation is transaction dependent. Whether you intend to gift to family, sell to a strategic buyer, sell to a management group, liquidate, or sell to a qualified employee ownership plan, realistic valuation will look vastly different in each scenario. "Everyone looking to buy a company is looking for cash flow," according to business transition/exit planner Michael Coffey, president of Corporate Capital Resources. He prompts business owners to begin their planning process by considering the following:

- *What do I want?*
- *What have I got to sell?*
- *Do I have something worth buying?*
- *If so, would somebody want to buy it? What is that buyer profile?*
- *What is the capacity to produce dividends?*

Michael underscores the criticality of complete and accurate financial reports, reviewed or even audited financials in some environments. He advises principals to tighten their bookkeeping, get accrual accounting in place, and know their numbers. "We find the greatest challenge for valuation models around financial performance: past, present, and future. You need something understandable that people can read."

Next, you need to be able to produce cogent projections on the outlook for your business, knowing that there are no perfect projections. You can start by defining the factors you control that most influence your company's value. It is preferable to show gradual and steady growth with good-quality earnings versus a choppy trend line. Demonstrating a solid forecast on the prospects for your customer base, your markets, and your industry is a valuable adjunct to a cogent earnings history.

THE MOST IMPORTANT SCORE

These days, the new benchmark for an income statement is EBIDTA, a sexier way to look at revenue that takes out non-operating items such as interest and ignores depreciation, amortization, and taxes. (Thus, the acronym EBIDTA is derived from *earnings before interest, depreciation, taxes, and amortization.*) For the valuation of private companies, a range of EBIDTA earnings multipliers can be expected, dependent on several factors such as industry, geography, and revenue. When looking at internal transactions of private company sales to management, Michael reports that valuations can range from five to six times EBIDTA.

You can begin to get a realistic idea of your business's market value by considering EBIDTA as a proxy for cash flow. All too often, what you think your business is worth is not what a willing buyer will pay for it. Most private and closely held business owners mistakenly assume they will get top dollar for their business. They fail to consider potential market changes, industry, economy, or unintended urgency (unpreparedness) to sell.

Attaining and maintaining complete accrual financials, complemented with regular scorecard data, additionally allows your company to be readily poised to seize opportunities; up-to-date financials avoid the need to scramble should they be required for a sale to third parties, mergers, acquisitions, or loans for capital expenditures. With an integrated strategy built over three to five, preferably even ten years, you will build a runway to have a smooth takeoff—and get the highest value when you do.

HIGO PAYS HIGH DIVIDENDS

Having a HIGO (house in good order) is a deliberate process and comprises a lot of basic financial planning, astute tax planning (and leveraging), and documentation. Understanding the importance of tax rules and timing is critical to the process. A HIGO probably includes a portfolio of financial vehicles such as wills, trusts, powers of attorney, life insurance (individually owned or owned by a trust), investments, pension and profit-sharing plans, real estate holdings, and advanced medical directives.

Remember to integrate plans and revisit them often. Normally, such implements are developed at different times, so consider all that can change over a few short years: personal and family dynamics, tax laws, the economy, business plans, and even your life goals. Having a HIGO makes you a high-profile target for a buyer and allows you to negotiate from a position of strength.

To do that, however, you will need some assistance because you don't know what you don't know. There are many mechanisms and financial vehicles to get you where you need to go. To achieve the highest outcome, build a team of trusted advisors who bring a depth of experience that will strengthen your company's unique position. Their knowledge, insight, and objectivity can be invaluable in keeping you focused, realistic, protected, and safeguarded against the unknown.

To illustrate, the IRS publishes a fifty-four-page guide for small businesses on how to pay their taxes. Yet there are 8,000 books on Amazon.com (for more than a million pages) on minimizing or avoiding paying taxes. So, for my part, I want to be engaged with someone who at least has some level of understanding of the million pages.[21]

Look for people who are idea-oriented and abundance thinkers. Know how everyone is compensated. You want to partner with someone keen to understand your process and thinking. Professionals who strive first to learn about your singular situation, your values, and your goals. Your overriding objective should be to create a *custom, integrated financial business plan.* You may be surprised at how beneficial one focused conversation with the right planning team can be to point your firm in the right direction.

RIGHT-HAND, LEFT-HAND SYNCHRONY

The exposure of not keeping your professional advisors working in concert, or at least being aware of your overall financial interests and implements, can hardly be overstated. Particularly for companies that have successfully navigated ever-increasing levels of complexity, change can create unintended consequences and present new conditions not previously considered. For example, we worked with owners of a century-old company who could not accept a $50 million offer for real estate they owned because it was in the wrong corporate structure. They would have netted fifty cents on the dollar, or less, had they proceeded. Do you think this company would have benefited from a roundtable discussion among their advisors and the owners?

A good place to start may be to have advisors submit a written report at least once a year to provide data for your sign-off, the audit. That will serve as their pledge that they have you covered. Typically, the CPA has been the lead advisor tasked with ensuring you pay the right amount of taxes. Their data would likely be based on historical data. In contrast, tax planning looks up to five years ahead. Still, it may provide a broader perspective on your accounting practices and upcoming tax laws, incorporating bigger-picture changes than you anticipated for your business. A collaboration process with integrity serves you best.

A similar scenario could play out with your legal advisors as well. Whether it's a general counsel, tax, or real estate attorney, they wait for direction, no matter how competent and responsive to your requests. The idea is to have the financial and legal advisors confer with one another on your behalf, being proactive and creative about best serving the company's interest. If your advisors are not privy to your master plan and an overview of the strategies to achieve it, you could risk harm or disservice to your firm. "Visual graphs and pictures are worth a thousand words."

WORKING *ON* YOUR BUSINESS

Knowing your numbers and getting your HIGO is directly related to the success of your business. It is not just about the far-off future; it's about building your wealth around your company's value. You undoubtedly have myriad demands and day-to-day pressures; consider permitting yourself to think about preparing for your endgame. Are you going to build your own buyer (internally) or find a buyer? Both have different implications and shared components. It has a direct bearing on the priorities of today for you and your business. By applying discipline now to keep your eyes on the prize, you will enhance business value exponentially.

Prudent planning also will account for TIME: *taxes, inflation, mistakes, and emergencies.* Those inevitable occurrences are smaller than a black swan event yet may throw a wrench in the works of normal operations, pumping the brakes on your well-considered plans. A company with mature simplicity can exhibit resiliency in a situation that would send a less prepared business reeling. Even better is to become "antifragile," as described by Nassim Taleb in his latest book.[22]

The bottom line is that you need to understand the numbers to know where you stand today, how the company trends from the past, and how well it tracks for the future. Knowing how your financial picture today comports with your long-range financial goals gives you a solid footing for planning and building the culture to create a lasting enterprise that can attain your highest aspirations.

APPLYING POSSIBILITY THINKING
Understand Your Numbers

1. Cultivate a high comfort level with your firm's balance sheet. Ask questions and resolve to discern the implications of changing influences in your accounting reports. Stay knowledgeable about trends and closely monitor the factors you deem to affect company value greatly.

2. Implement a scorecard of nine to twelve indices to report in and communicate the status of your key performance indicators. Receive and review at the same time each week to strategize near-term actions around areas of concern. Remember to include historical trending data and year-to-date progress/regress for each category, and if desired, color code for ease of reference.

3. Remember that business continuity planning directly informs company value. Decide to clarify your vision for your endgame and your company's financial future, then assess how you will proceed to a strong

---

roadmap that will protect and enhance the value of your enterprise.

4. Tighten up your financial reporting system to ensure complete and accurate financial reports, with accrual accounting for a solid grasp of your historical and current balance sheets. Well-considered projections are an important asset in planning, so it's wise to be circumspect and include forecasts for your customer base, markets, and industry.

5. Analyze your EBIDTA and think of it as a proxy for cash flow. Learn how to assess the potential value of your company realistically. Complete and current financials allow you to seize opportunities more readily, be it a sale to third parties, mergers, acquisitions, or loans for capital expenditures.

6. Commit to having a HIGO. Review and integrate all the instruments in your portfolio. Realize that you need a team of trusted advisors who can alert you to pitfalls and opportunities. Arrange for them to coordinate and confer on your behalf.

7. Permit yourself to work on your business; it's the most important thing you can do to build and protect its value. When you stay above the fray at least half the time, you gain perspective to keep your eyes on a bigger prize.

SOMETHING TO THINK ABOUT

PART III

WHAT
COMES
NEXT

*The quality of everything we do
depends on the quality
of the thinking we do first.*

*The quality of our thinking
depends on the way
we treat each other
while we are thinking.*

—**NANCY KLINE**, *A Time to Think* [30]

9

THEN, CREATE THE CULTURE

If I were to tell you how much the advice of my mentor, Chief Nesbit, influenced my life, it would fill another book. His wisdom and witticisms were legendary among all who knew him. One of my favorites was his use of a simple prop that he employed when recruiting or discussing teamwork. He would offer a pencil to the individual and ask them to break it, which they easily did. Then Chief would hand them a bundle of pencils he had rubber-banded together and ask them to break it. Naturally, this was not possible. He would then sit back and kindly explain, "To achieve greatness requires joint work and being part of a team."

When a prospective client told him no, they weren't interested, he regarded it as simply a response about needing more information—whether it was he or they who needed more clarity. Asking questions was one of Chief's greatest gifts. He knew he could not help someone unless his questions required them to think. Seeking clarity allows wise choices. Chief forged strong partnerships with his clients and never stopped asking them clarifying questions: He believed that thinking big mattered in changing people's hopes and dreams. His guiding belief was that he was ensuring people's lives for a bigger tomorrow, and he pursued that mission with vigor.

CREATE YOUR OWN THINK TANK

Often, we are unaware of our untrue but self-limiting assumptions. That's how incisive questions can unleash new avenues of insight. Financial Designs employs the *Time to Think* methodology based on Nancy Kline's pioneering system, The Thinking Environment. It is an integral part of all our engagements with clients because we want to clarify and confirm that we understand what the client has on their mind and what they're thinking about. It begins with asking a provocative question, giving a client our full attention, and allowing them to be the thinker. It's our way of getting owners to start reflecting on: *What do you care about? What matters most? What do you want to see happen?*[23]

When leaders have clear answers to these core questions, they can view them as touchstones to frame most everything in that context and articulate it incessantly. This promotes enculturation throughout the firm, as team members also embrace and embody these core values. It brings goals to life and becomes a corporate manifesto that is not a paper tiger but a living culture of a unified vision.

Putting the puzzle together without the picture on the box is much harder and takes longer. Try thinking of your key messages as providing the picture of what teams are building toward so they may proceed in a systemic, inspiring way. Then they know where they are compared to the picture and work together to achieve it.

YOU CREATE THE CULTURE

Have you created a de facto culture in your firm or one that is well considered and thoughtfully instilled? Here is where you can assess your level of self-awareness. Nothing changes without it, and self-awareness leads to self-mastery. As your firm's standard bearer, you set the direction and tone for the entire enterprise. Is that emphasis in resonance with your intentions?

Ask yourself: do you have a culture of goal setting? One of accountability? Is it a culture of alignment? Do you have a culture of openness where anyone can speak truth to power? Is it a culture of ownership thinking?

According to *Harvard Business Review*, employees seek workplaces that align with their beliefs. Quoting survey results from the National Bureau of Economic Research, *HBR* asserts that employees care decidedly about a company's culture and seek a common vision of purpose and success.

The survey found that nine out of ten CFOs believe improving company culture would increase their business value and performance. The article continues:

> *As leaders grapple with how to recruit top candidates and retain employees, they must rethink how they're shaping and building a culture that unites people around a common cause. Great culture should provide continuous alignment to the vision, purpose, and goals of the organization.*
>
> *Leaders may believe they're putting in the work to build and improve, but the reality is that employees don't agree. Nearly half of employees (45 percent) say leadership is minimally or not at all committed to improving culture. This discrepancy can lead to harrowing business repercussions, such as voluntary turnover that can cost organizations up to two times an employee's annual salary.* [24, 25]

Employees vote with their feet, and it is too late the day they vote not to come in. Now, remember that people quit twice. The first time, they just quit without speaking. The second time is when they tell you. Hopefully, there are not more than two weeks in between. Because if it is more than that, you have a big problem. Your system is getting infected by a virus, which ultimately results in the exit of the virus. Although it's now out, you may not be able to cure the damage it has wrought easily. Culture *matters.*

HIGH-FUNCTIONING TEAMS

Socratic business advisor and author Jim Collins, in his book, *Good to Great: Why Some Companies Make the Leap and Others Don't,* candidly shares that his extensive research did not support his theories about what makes businesses transform successfully. He expected to confirm that the first step in taking a company to the next level would be to set a new direction, vision, and strategy and then get everyone committed and aligned behind the new direction. Instead, he found the reverse: frontrunners prioritized the people part of the equation. He writes: "They said, in essence, 'If we get the right people on the bus, the right people in the right seats, and the wrong people off the bus, then we'll figure out how to take it someplace great.'"[26]

The trick may lie in developing and empowering an entrepreneurial team by involving them in crucial conversations and incentivizing them appropriately. Such team members are not entrepreneurs, though they adopt the mindset of owners, not renters. An entrepreneurial team understands what their role is and the benefit to them when they succeed. They are vested in the company's achievements. You must avoid NETMA at all costs. Nobody Ever Tells Me Anything.

EMPLOYEES AS BUSINESS PARTNERS

Investing in human capital by deciding that people are more important than equipment or supplies will supercharge your succession management plan. Case in point: a client of ours who believes in putting money into people brought in an executive and paid him 50 percent more than managers in the company thought was equitable. This caused discord and frustration over what was perceived as the new hire's inflated salary. The owner stood firm, however, abiding by his decision to forge a different direction with outside talent. Together, they turned the company around, doubling revenues in a year and a half.

It's human nature that absent a vision larger than themselves, people are likely to view opportunities from the perspective of WIIFM—*what's in it for me?* At Financial Designs, we've discovered that the key is to provide employees the IP—irrefutable proof—that if the company is successful, then key management and all employees will benefit. With the right planning, we design programs that drive people to align with the company owner's vision and purpose. It's a win-win-win for the business, the employees, and the primary shareholders.

Viewing human capital as your most valued asset can have long-term advantages. An integrated, high-functioning team is a powerful operational advantage that an outside buyer will find compelling, if not imperative. As part of the purchase agreement, some buyers may require employees in essential sales, production, and management positions to maintain their employment with the company for a specified period. Because the value of a firm is not all about customer lists and hard assets, a solid culture can deliver substantial recompense.

CRAFTING CORE VALUES

Your company will need to create its values. Failure to do so creates culture by default. Every business has a culture that results from deliberate creation or unconscious evolution. To get your thinking kickstarted about what you'd like to envision as aspirational values for your company, try some on for size and start to imagine how they can be refined and tailored to your culture.

Below are Nancy Kline's ten components of The Thinking Environment. *Time to Think* has identified "ten behaviors that generate the finest independent thinking," according to Kline. "In the presence of these ten behaviors, people think for themselves with rigor, imagination, courage, and grace." The components are:

- Attention
- Equality
- Ease
- Appreciation
- Encouragement
- Feelings
- Information
- Difference
- Incisive Questions
- Place [27]

We employ these components in our work with clients. We find that it assists them in overcoming resistance and opening to possibility thinking. While there is a plethora of information about crafting corporate values, best practices indicate that powerful core values are often around abundance, recognition and reward, transparency, and trust.

THE DRIVE TO SUCCESS

One of Financial Designs' strategic partners, Chuck Richards, of ValueCompass and CoreValue Advisor software, has developed a synthesis of operational performance drivers that most influence business maturation and growth—and hence, prosperity. It's a framework that ValuCompass believes can measure the operating business engine to maximize traction by analyzing vulnerabilities and identifying the place of most potential. Chuck asserts that "efficient operations, ensured by strategic management of the eighteen drivers, will produce optimal shareholder value and a culture of success."

18 DRIVERS OF
OPERATIONAL PERFORMANCE

Market Drivers

- Growth
- Large Potential Market
- Dominant Market Share
- Recurring Revenue
- Barriers To Entry

- Customer Diversification
- Product Differentiation
- Brand
- Margin Advantage

Operational Drivers

- Company Overview
- Financial
- Sales & Marketing
- Operations
- Customer Satisfaction

- Senior Management
- Human Resources
- Legal
- Innovation

THE CRUCIAL MISSING INGREDIENT

I firmly believe that if business owners aren't doing the deep dive but are just paddling along the surface of day-to-day operations (and hassles), they're missing out in a big way and hindering their future. At the end of the day, sure, you must demonstrate good performance; no one can argue that because your revenue reflects how well your business is doing financially. Yet it's not the only (or perhaps even the best) benchmark.

Does your organization have good mental health? If you are not having *fun*, why are you doing it? Why are you enduring the long hours and the stress? Where is your sense of making a difference, of leaving a meaningful contribution to the world? These are not flippant questions. They impinge on the whole megillah because no one should have to choose between profit and purpose.

Take Walt, a doctor who heads a successful medical practice group. At sixty-three, Walt suddenly talks about retiring in six months. So, we listen, and we ask questions about this. He is frustrated because he has managed the group for many years to benefit the patients and the physicians. Now, when he wants to do things differently, he is encountering resistance from his partners. Add to this the sobering reality that over the past several years, a number of doctors either left, died, or got sick unexpectedly. That was a wake-up call for Walt.

"You're not having any fun, are you?" we queried him.

"What do you mean?" he asked, puzzled.

"The visit on the blue planet is short, so are you having any *fun*?"

"No," he said flatly. "I guess not."

I showed him our simple circle diagram representing all the parameters that go into business achievement. It's a circle but not a closed loop; it has a gap. Because no company can possibly have a 360-degree circle, there's always something, some room for improvement (and there are usually a few blind spots, too). That gap illustrates the missing ingredient.

For Walt and many business owners like him, that ingredient is *fun*. Some call it purpose, a mission, flow, enthusiasm, or making a difference. We prefer to think of it as having fun. So why not track the firm's fun meter as one of your KPIs? Find your fun and make fun a core value, and your company's culture will take on a whole new dimension.

APPLYING POSSIBILITY THINKING
Then, Create The Culture

1. Determine what value you put on the people part of your company's equation. Do you really appreciate the value of your team? Consider how much attention and emphasis you place on your company's culture.

2. Reflect on the essential questions: *What do you care about? What matters most? What do you want to see happen?* Your answers are the touchstones of context and communication about your core values.

3. Determine what kind of culture you presently have and think about how you have created it, by intent or by default. Consider becoming more aware of how culture influences employee retention and achievement.

4. Question whether you have the right people in place and whether they function as an empowered, entrepreneurial team that understands their role and how they stand to benefit from their efforts and the success of the whole.

5. Provide employees with irrefutable proof of the significance of their contribution through meaningful incentives. See the long-term advantages of regarding human capital as your company's most valued asset. Build a solid culture that will pay dividends for years ahead and benefit an outside buyer and loyal successors within the firm.

6. Deliver optimal shareholder value by developing a culture of achievement guided by the eighteen drivers of operational success. Use them to maximize traction by analyzing vulnerabilities and identifying the areas with the most potential.

7. Ask yourself if you are missing the essential ingredient of fun. If you are, why are you working? Reflect on your motivations and determine if fun is the missing ingredient in your company's culture.

SOMETHING TO THINK ABOUT

10

INTO THE FUTURE

Your future is abundant.

Here's how I know: you are reading this. You have started considering your thoughts and decided to have a visionary, abundant mindset. You're done thinking about your business from a scarcity point of view when you believe that business is a scrappy competition for finite resources. You no longer worry about your business getting a piece of the pie; now, you focus on how your company will upgrade processes to make more pies.

There is no fun in scarcity. It can fester, unacknowledged, and infect the rest of your organization. It reflects in how people delegate, how they hire, which opportunities they pursue (or neglect), and in most of the decisions they make. Here's the thing: it's almost always *illusory*. Scarcity is in people's imagination, and it is not even real—and that can be a major stumbling block. Adopting an abundant mindset requires considerable dedication every day because scarcity is always waiting to pounce, hovering to convince you that *"you don't have the money, you don't have the time, you lack the experience, no one in your family has ever done this before."* Yadda, yadda, yadda. Resistance.

According to *Inc.* magazine, the key to creating a lens through which you view the world in abundance lies in the belief that you can create what you want. Empowered leaders see everything as an opportunity instead of a challenge or defeat.

They are curious, and they surround themselves with other abundant thinkers. They can flip perspectives to a positive point of view: adventure versus change, opportunities versus challenges, growth and learning versus failure.[28]

Abundance is where the fun is, where the action is; it brings out the art of possibility. Abundance changes your brain chemistry; it is energy giving. It taps into your unique abilities, allowing you to exercise judgment. It gives you a chance to see people smile, to give someone a hand up, not a handout. It cultivates generosity, which intrinsically feeds you and everyone around you.

THE FUTURE OF PROSPERITY

At Financial Designs, we work with our clients to create compensation programs that do not cost the company money. This is a trend that we predict will expand in the next five to ten years as private and family business owners realize that shared revenue would not even be possible without their team's efforts. By creating the right compensation structures, you allow people to win. It's like the adage: *capitalism is a good system, though you better have some capitalists in that system.*

Consider creating a process of mutual benefit that serves the employees, executives, and shareholders. See if it doesn't permeate throughout the culture, as employees become more focused on productivity and working together to attain goals rather than on office politics and gamesmanship.

There's an old fable about the three masons, and I tell it for a reason. A man walks up to each of the three independently as they are working and asks each one the same question: "What are you doing?"

The first mason spits on the ground, looks at the man, and says, "I am laying bricks. What the hell does it look like I'm doing?"

The second mason groans and mops his brow, sighing, "I am building this wall—it's a living."

The third mason looks up, with light shining in his eyes, and says, "I am building a cathedral."

Which bricklayer works for you? The laborer who is putting in the hours, the builder who is focused on the job at hand, or the visionary intent on the pinnacle of his efforts? The third mason isn't just working a job. He has a calling. In his mind, he is building something significant that will make a difference. When you build a compensation plan with the appropriate transparency that aligns employees with shareholders to achieve outstanding results, you recognize and reward those who share the power of purpose.

If the company doesn't get a return on invested capital, there isn't anything to pay out. Once you've figured out the ROI—10, 15, or 20 percent—and it is achieved, you can distribute that revenue in retirement benefits. Determine a profit ratio to reward employees; it could be 80/20, 70/30, or 60/40. Our most successful client has historically paid out 25 to 40 percent of their profits.

THE FUTURE OF MANAGEMENT

Many private and family-owned businesses operate in a closed system. Aside from their stable of trusted advisors, they don't share information or discuss their affairs with anyone outside the company. (As we've examined, most don't share information with their advisor teams.) One of the trends we are encouraging clients to do is to install at least one outside board member. We are not talking about creating a board of advisors (operating principally in name only) but a fully-fledged member of the board of directors (voting). That is an entirely different level of governance, accountability, and transparency.

According to CoreValue Advisor Software, which has collected data on about 55,000 private and family businesses, 65 percent of companies want to grow their organization, 20 percent want to prepare their company for sale or succession, and 15 percent have no plan. This is an inflection point for companies built over the past twenty, thirty, or forty years. These businesses provide valuable goods and services; they are profitable and can't find someone to take them over. Thus, many are facing demise. Or resurgence.

We will likely see more and more small- to medium-sized business owners learning how to elevate themselves to the role of chairman by promoting or hiring a president to appoint and groom the next generation of executives and managers. Savvy owners are shaping their company's future well before they intend to step aside, their companies are thriving, and they are having fun doing it.

If you have big dreams, do you think it is time to start operating like you are in the big leagues?

THE FUTURE OF YOU

Having come this far and devoted so much of your time, talent, and treasury to your company, it is high time you start thinking about maximizing the return on those investments. If you've begun to rise above the tyranny of the urgent and to think beyond the immediate (or at least farther out than next quarter), you are off to a roaring start. When you begin questioning your priorities, you become self-aware, allowing you to marshal your thoughts and elevate your mindset. Should you find your personality changing to be more optimistic, generous, and forward-thinking than you were before, you are well on your way to mastery.

Dedicating more of your thoughts and energy to possibility inspires you to plan for your abundant future. Then you will derive fulfillment from working *on* your business, not just *in* it. In so doing, you will learn, expand, and develop new confidence in your management abilities. By discovering different ways to approach your work and broadening your scope beyond it, you may start to assess how you benefit and influence key stakeholders, employees, your family, and your community. The world will be a better place for the difference you are making.

THE FUTURE OF AGILE THINKING

Hopefully, you've started to think more about the synergy of left- and right-brain thinking. Synthesizing practical, logical planning with possibility and creativity will propel your administration to the next level. Clarity about where you want to take your company is the first step in designing priorities and plans to guide you there. Just like having the picture on the puzzle box to compare with the puzzle pieces before you, key performance indicators will benchmark progress on your way. That will make you more comfortable shifting your focus from immediate to long-term goals. Now you can embrace letting go by delegating more and concentrating on hiring and developing your company's leaders of tomorrow.

Regarding your business from a higher perspective and becoming more thoughtful about your aspirations will naturally encourage your personal development as a motivating leader. When you do that, you will undoubtedly become more aware of how and what you communicate. Which messages best articulate your goals and galvanize employees to achieve them?

When you dive deeper to study your financial picture and comprehend your financials, you will build confidence that you have the plans to provide a solid foundation. You will have done what you can to prepare for the unexpected. Moreover, you will have forged resilience to shore up the business during challenges or readily capitalize on new opportunities.

Contemplating the present—and future—value of your company is multifactorial. Success(ion) planning is mandatory if you want your business to continue after you step aside or sell. Recruiting and developing capable and committed leaders is key, as are developing core values and a culture that will stand the test of time. An abundance mindset will serve you extraordinarily well, as will your generosity with the employees who make it all possible. None of these factors can be developed overnight. They take foresight, planning, and enculturation.

THE FUTURE OF THINKING DIFFERENTLY

"How we think shows through in how we act," wrote David J. Schwartz in *The Magic of Thinking Big*. "Attitudes are mirrors of the mind. They reflect thinking."[29]

Here's hoping you have been prompted to analyze your thinking and consider new ways of thinking differently: expansively, imaginatively, and abundantly. May you eagerly undertake the adventure of exploring new perspectives, petitioning outside viewpoints, and broadening your depth of knowledge.

So, the next time someone catches you gazing out the window, lost in thought, don't blush—you're likely doing the most important work of all.

APPLYING POSSIBILITY THINKING
Into The Future

---

1. Choose a visionary, abundant mindset, knowing it is a decision you may have to commit to often. Remember that scarcity is illusory, and it is always waiting to creep back into your thoughts and argue for your limitations.

2. Believe that abundance is where the fun is and that it cultivates generosity, which intrinsically rewards you and everyone around you. It gives you a chance to enrich your company and your world.

3. Look into creating revenue-sharing programs that don't technically cost the firm, yet forge loyalty and vested interest in the organization's success. Realize

how it will influence the culture when employees have a stake in meeting stretch goals and advancing the business.

4. Weigh the benefits of installing at least one outside board member with full advisory and voting privileges. Consider how it will formalize and elevate corporate governance and shift transparency and accountability.

5. Get serious about preparing your firm for succession and its transition well ahead of schedule. Elevate your role to chairman and appoint (and mentor) a president who will begin to assume more administrative and leadership roles and develop a management team to step up.

6. Refine and analyze your thought processes and leadership practices across the disciplines of visioning, planning, communicating, leading, and financial preparedness. Be cognizant that appropriate foresight, planning, and enculturation take time; it's not an overnight process.

7. Make time to think. Then observe how you think. Is it expansive? Imaginative? Abundant? Explore new perspectives, seek outside opinions, and always keep learning.

SOMETHING TO THINK ABOUT

APPENDICES

A: ACKNOWLEDGMENTS

Many individuals played a role in bringing this book to life. Some offered inspiration and support while others offered business experience and a shared tenacity for abundance thinking.

To the following friends, colleagues, and supporters, I say thank you: Tommy Battle, Mike Berry, Bill Bishop, Tim Blanks, Daryl Bryant, Bob Burke, Maurice Clark, Michael Coffey, David Cohn, Mark Dorman, Micah De Salvio, George Eudailey, Diane Garmey, Jason Grantz, Bill Gust, Chuck Hollander, Penny Hatcher, Josh Hazelwood, Adam Holt, Cheryl Johnson, Hough Johnson, Greg Kasten MD, Al Kingan, Nancy Kline, Ron Lovelace, Ford Mays, Jim McCabe, Todd McGee, Chuck McGinnis, Kevin Mulhern, Chief Nesbit, Pat Olearcek, Kevin Paasch, Gerald Radican, Chuck Richards, Jim Richards, Mike Roberts, Ralph Sabine, Tommy Schaff, Paul Scioli, Sarah Scruggs-Reddell, Joe Sparacio, Dave Stephens, Pete Swisher, Bruce Tanahill, Mike Thelen, Gary Thacker, Brian Trazinski, Dan Tuckwiller, John Vaccaro, Kathryn Wakefield, Edmond Walters, Vera Waters, Peck Whitcomb, Jackie Wiggins, Tina Witt.

Special thanks to Tommy Schaff for encouraging me to write this book. Further acknowledgements are extended to my children and grandchildren for their abundant futures:

Courtney and Medford Sorrells (Winifred and Smith), Sarah and Matt Reddell, Evan and Kate Sumner, Sara and Charles Busch (Brooks).

This book is dedicated to my wife, Kandy.

B: ABOUT THE AUTHOR

Rick Scruggs is the founder/CEO of a company called Financial Designs. The company's financial advisors work with private and family business owners and their teams who want to create a business asset. This transferable enterprise will thrive after the owner exits. He is passionate about his purpose: speaking candidly with people about love, health, finances, and business ownership. For more than forty-five years, he has made it his mission to coach and encourage family business owners, business partners, and corporate management on how to think about their businesses. Financial Designs works with business owners on continuity, success(ion), transition, and exit planning. Rick's dedication to and focus on his clients is, in his view, the same commitment and focus they show for their businesses and families. His work is more than a career; it drives him, and that passion is clearly demonstrated in everything he does for his clients.

Rick created The Vision Advocate Experience and the Owner's Advantage Program twenty years ago and has since co-created The Abundance Business Coaching Program with Tommy Battle and Sarah Scruggs-Reddell. Rick is a registered representative of and offers securities, investment advisory services, and financial planning through MML Investors Services, LLC and has been a registered advisor with MassMutual for over forty-five years. He is one of the founding members of the Legacy Advisor Network, whose independent advisors serve private and family business owners with a network of advisors. Financial Designs is an advisor to client assets totaling over $1 billion. Financial Designs offers a full-service approach to the qualified plans arena, from plan design consultation to employee meetings, education, and overall plan compliance. Rick is a graduate of the *401(k) Coach* and the *Retirement Advisor University* program through UCLA Business School and holds his CKP designation. His daughter, Sarah Scruggs-Reddell, RIPC, is an advisor/partner and runs the retirement plan operations. In 2022, she was named a NAPA Top 50 Female Retirement Plan Advisor.

Rick lives with his wife, Kandy, in Forest, Virginia.

C: ENDNOTES

1 Z. Christopher Mercer, *Unlocking Private Company Wealth: Proven Strategies And Tools For Managing Wealth In Your Private Business* (Brockton, MA: Peabody Publishing, LP, 2014).

2 Stephen R. Covey, *The Seven Habits of Highly Effective People: Powerful Lessons in Personal Change* (New York: Simon and Schuster, 1989).

3 Covey, *Seven Habits.*

4 Greg McKeown, *Essentialism: The Disciplined Pursuit Of Less* (New York: Crown Business, 2014).

5 "Delegating: A Huge Management Challenge for Entrepreneurs," Gallup, 14 April 2015 accessed June 11, 2021, https://news.gallup.com/businessjournal/182414/delegating-huge-management-challenge-entrepreneurs.aspx.

6 Dan Sullivan, *The Self-Managing Company: Freeing Yourself Up From Everything That Prevents You From Creating a 10x Better Future* (Powell, Ohio: Academy Elite, 2020).

7 Joseph Campbell, *The Hero with a Thousand Faces* (New York: Pantheon Books, 1949).

8 Dan Sullivan, *Who Not How: The Formula To Achieve Bigger Goals Through Accelerating Teamwork* (Carlsbad, CA: Hay House Business, 2020).

9 John Hall, "The Cost of Turnover Can Kill Your Business and Make Things Less Fun," *Forbes,* 9 May 2019, accessed April 22, 2021, https://www.forbes.com/sites/johnhall/2019/05/09/the-cost-of-turnover-can-kill-your-business-and-make-things-less-fun/.

10 Bob Proctor, *You Were Born Rich: Now You Can Discover and Develop Those Riches* (Scottsdale: Life Success Productions, 1984).

11 Edward de Bono, *Six Thinking Hats: An Essential Approach to Business Management* (Boston: Little Brown and Company, 1985).

12 Jim Collins and Jerry I. Porras, *Built to Last: Successful Habits of Visionary Companies* (New York: Harper Business, 2004).

13 Nassim Nicholas Taleb, *The Black Swan: The Impact of the Highly Improbable* (New York: Random House, 2007).

14 Nassim Nicholas Taleb, *Antifragile: Things That Gain From Disorder* (New York: Random House, 2012).

15 "Titanic: The Unsinkable Ship," accessed May 3, 2021, https://www.titanicuniverse. com/titanic-the-unsinkable-ship/1443.

16 Simon Sinek, *How Great Leaders Inspire Action,* TED.com, September 2009, accessed July 7, 2021, https://www.ted.com/talks/simon_sinek_how_great_leaders_inspire_action.

17 Simon Sinek, *Start With Why: How Great Leaders Inspire Everyone to Take Action* (London: Portfolio, 2009).

18 Kim Gerard, "It's Not Nagging: Why Persistent, Redundant Communication Works," Harvard Business School Working Knowledge, April 18, 2011, https:// hbswk.hbs.edu/item/its-not-nagging-why-persistent-redundant-communication-works.

19 Eric Schmidt and Jonathan Rosenberg, *How Google Works* (New York: Grand Central Publishing, 2014).

20 Stephen A. Schwarzman, *What It Takes: Lessons in the Pursuit of Excellence* (New York: Avid Reader Press / Simon & Schuster, 2019).

21 "Tax Guide for Small Business," accessed August 5, 2021, https://www.irs.gov/pub/ irs-pdf/p334.pdf.

22 Taleb, *Antifragile.*

23 "Ten Components of The Thinking Environment," accessed August 6, 2021, https:// www.timetothink.com/thinking-environment/the-ten-components/.

24 Natalie Baumgartner, "Build A Culture That Aligns With People's Values," *Harvard Business Review*, April 8, 2020, https://hbr.org/2020/04/build-a-culture-that-aligns-with-peoples-values.

25 "Corporate Culture: Evidence from the Field," National Bureau of Economic Research, March 2017, https://www.nber.org/papers/w23255.

26 Jim Collins, *Good to Great: Why Some Companies Make the Leap and Others Don't* (New York: Harper Business, 2001).

27 "The Ten Components."

28 Kyle Gogeun, "The Importance of an Abundant Mindset for Business Leaders," *Inc.*, August 16, 2019, https://www.inc.com/young-entrepreneur-council/the-importance-of-an-abundance-mindset-for-business-leaders.html.

29 David J. Schwartz, Ph.D., *The Magic of Thinking Big* (New York: Simon & Schuster, 1959).

30 Nancy Kline, *Time to Think* (London: Cassell, 2015).

D: INDEX